How to
Lead Your Life with
7 Treasures
You Own!

The Art of Living!

Farima Wassel Joya

Printed in the United States of America

ISBN-13: 978-0615743400 (7 Treasures Press)
ISBN-10: 0615743404

7 Treasures Press
7tPress@farimawassel.com
(510) 819-9330

10 9 8 7 6 5 4 3 2

This book is dedicated to all my fellow Afghans in Afghanistan and abroad.

Acknowledgement

First and foremost, I am in debt to my husband, Jamshed Joya, because without his support and encouragement, this book would not have been completed. I would also like to thank my daughter, Sahar, my son, Suhrab, my family & community for their support. I am also grateful to Mr. Abdul Salam Shayek Faraz and Mr. Sedique Popal for their wonderful forewords to this book.

About the Book

This book makes it easy for you to make decisions based on principles that you will not regret later in life. By following the 7 Treasures principles, you will be empowered to lead your own life. If life is like a blank canvas, then this book will empower you to paint your own picture. When all is done, you will be looking at a masterpiece that you have created and you will be proud of your accomplishments.

By depositing into our own natural 7 Treasures of **health, feelings, knowledge, faith, family, career, and wealth**, you will look at your life events from a different perspective. You will take responsibility for your own actions and decisions, pass life obstacles with ease and courage, and look forward to living your life as you imagined it in your dreams.

This book is put together as a result of my search for happiness. I found my peace of mind and satisfaction by minding my own treasures. I have consciously followed this philosophy for the past decade. Now, I'd like to share it with you. I hope that it becomes as effective in your life as much as it is in mine.

Table of Contents

Foreword

I was enthralled by Mrs. Joya's book "Seven Treasures." This highly educational book casts its rays of light so widely to the eyes of those whose lives are occupied by despair and darkness.

With the depth of her vision of life, the author made her extremely intellectual observation on our personal and social lives. She sees treasures on our path. These treasures are invisible to us because the dust of low self-esteem has hidden them from our view. We do not know these precious treasures, and we do not realize they're God given bounties that were given to us with no cost. We are living in the dark of afflictions without knowing our own powers of imagination. Reading this book will help us see and value those treasures. Without them, we are not only deprived from a higher quality of life but we lose our physical and psychological health and live miserable lives.

Treasures are desired because they can give us happiness and satisfaction. Whatever else that gives the same, deserves to be called treasures.

This book proves that these seven things can give us as much happiness as any treasure plus freedom of mind from distractions. I congratulate Mrs. Joya for this book and wish her the best success for her future works.

Abdul Salam Shayak Faraz
Afghan Author and Poet
Sunnyvale, California

Foreword

I read and tremendously enjoyed this very informative, intriguing, and well-researched book. It chronicles in great detail how working towards and owning the seven treasures of health, feelings, knowledge, faith, family, career, and wealth can pave the way for one's success and peace of mind. By reading different chapters of the book, one can infer that the author, in very subtle way, believes in the very famous American proverb, "Success is 99% perspiration and 1% luck." In other words, she encourages her readers to work hard to earn these treasures.

It is my hope that the readers take Mrs. Farima Wassel Joya's message seriously and work hard to earn these seven treasures in order to be both happy and successful.

Dr. Sedique Popal
Professor of Linguistics
University of San Francisco
San Francisco, California

About The Author

Considering where I could be today had I never left Afghanistan, I think of myself as one of the luckiest women in the world. I have been living in Northern California for the past twenty-five years with my family and loving every minute of it. My husband, Jamshed Joya, is my childhood sweetheart and my biggest fan. My daughter, Sahar, just graduated as an interior designer from the Academy of Art University in San Francisco and is married to a wonderful man, Tamim Assifi. My son, Suhrab, is eighteen, and already dreaming of owning his own unique business.

I am trying hard to keep current on technology and trends for broadcasting personal, business, and inspirational stories. I challenge myself every day to be a better person and to live according to the 7 Treasures principles. I have always lived a balanced life and found happiness from inside out, and it started when I was a child back in Afghanistan.

As a teenager, I always argued with my father over the value of money. My father, a shop owner, is a hard worker who saw providing money as the greatest measure of success and happiness, and was very proud of providing for his large family. I always wanted to prove him wrong, and this is why I always looked at creative and alternative ways to find happiness.

I arrived in the United States as an Afghan refugee in 1987 with my husband and one-year-old daughter. We were put on Welfare right away. After a couple of months of finding ourselves, we started working and had nothing but the hope of living an American dream life. For a good decade, we were in survival mode in a total strange country with new laws, language, and culture.

People regularly come to the United States with a dream of being rich and famous. I, on the other hand, had never wished to have lots of money. I believed, and still believe today, that having lots of money without discipline and wisdom brings danger and unhappiness. I like the challenge of finding creative ways to live comfortably without hard work.

My challenge was to experience the many opportunities that this country has to offer. The possibility to change careers and do different things for a living, to freely choose what to do for yourself is something found only in the United States, and I would be a fool for not trying many things. In return, I got some experience and knowledge that would not have been possible had I not taken risks to explore this new life.

My first training was in a business school learning to be a word processing operator. I had some fascination with computers, and at the time, this was the closest thing that would bring me to a computer. Shortly after that, I had to take additional English classes in order to keep my job, and I did.

For the next ten years, I kept my job and went to school for an Associate Degree in Entrepreneurship and Management. All of my classes, such as accounting, business plan, marketing, graphic design, business law, were taken on a need basis in order to help my husband with his one man business.

I had good benefits and job security working as a word processor for the County of Marin, California, but I was frustrated with the lack of opportunity. I thought that there must be more to life than sitting at the same desk year after year and typing for a living. I quit my job.

Next, I found myself working with my husband in the signs and graphics business. His small warehouse shop moved to a prominent location and was doing really well. I was happy to work with computers and business owners. We sold the business at its peak.

Afterward, we invested the money in two businesses: a fast food restaurant and an import business. For a while we worked two jobs, long hours on a crazy fast paced basis. I ran the restaurant for eight years until the lease expired. I was relieved. Around 2008, the economy was heading down. My husband and I both focused all of our attention on our art and frame import business, which eventually became a custom picture frame manufacturing business, our current source of income.

While working at the sign business, I was looking for more opportunities. A friend of mine sold some nutritional supplements to me, which I took for losing weight. I became involved with the sales rep and signed up as an associate. This business did not work for me right from the start, and I ended up giving away all of my investment.

A fifty-year-old Englishman named Paul came and joined us in the sign business for a short time. He was a world traveler and needed to work for some quick cash. Before he left, he gave me a book as a gift that changed my life. The book was, "A Touch of Greatness," by Frank Talbot.

I started my self-development learning from the world's most inspiring people through books and seminars. One of them is Donald Trump, the giant real estate developer and investor. When he was speaking at a conference in San Francisco, I had to go and see him up close. During the same seminar, I ended up buying a package of workbooks and sets of instructions, authored by Raymond Aaron, on how to design your own perfect life. This was when I felt the need to get out of the stresses of the fast food restaurant and a seven-day working week, because I figured I had other choices.

The most important thing that this package did for me was to make it clear what I wanted in my life. Once I knew what I wanted, I made up my mind and designed my life with my imagination, and wrote my action plan down on paper.

My next adventure was in real estate. I wanted to become a real estate investor and attended a costly seminar. I became an investor, but didn't continue it as a serious business. I started with full steam, but somehow could not convince my husband that it was a good thing for us to do. He never became interested, and I slowly lost my passion.

In the summer of 2008, I made a declaration that by July of next year, I would earn my living online. My next series of experiments was as follows: I bought a couple of packages about online businesses: specifically, on eBay and investing in the stock market. I tried both for a while, but could not keep up with online day trading. However, my time invested in the stock market proved to be a great learning experience for me.

I kept my eBay store and my ecommerce sites, which continue to do well for me even today. However, I am always looking for opportunities and push myself to do better every day.

I volunteered and became the president of a non-profit organization named the Berkeley Bamyan Education Foundation, www.bbefusa.org. The main goals of our organization are to help women and children with self-sufficiency in Afghanistan. We have offered vocational training in carpet weaving and sewing as well as literacy classes for the past five years.

Since the rise of the Afghan satellite TV stations here in the Bay Area, I have produced and hosted two one hour weekly shows in Farsi. The shows are broadcast online as well as through satellite receivers throughout the United States and Canada. This experience brought me closer to my community and the challenges that Afghans face abroad which lead me to further my education in media and communications.

In the fall of 2008, I signed up for a Multimedia Communications degree with the Academy of Art University in San Francisco on a part time basis. I am looking forward to graduating with my Bachelor of Art Degree in the summer of 2015.

My goal, which is beyond my wildest dreams, is to inspire you to take responsibility to lead your own life through the ups and downs of unpredictability and to find the art of living in your every-day routine.

Introduction

Why Do You Need To Lead?

You need to take charge of your own life because nobody else will do it for you. Most of us live a routine life that we carry on unconsciously or that others have set for us. As a result, we get old with many regrets. We get comfortable living in our routine and don't want to leave our comfort zone. If we don't take the lead, we may be cooked like a frog. A couple of scientists wanted to cook a frog, but as soon as they would put the frog in the hot water, it would jump out of the pot. So they decided to put the frog in a pot of cold water and start a fire under the pot. The frog was getting comfortable and the water was getting hot and hotter, and finally the frog was cooked. This is the danger of living in the comfort zone.

There are people who love their comfort zone and will not step out of it unless something happens to them. For instance, until they lose their job, get sick, or a natural disaster forces them out of their homes. This is when they suffer a great deal, until they find their comfort zone again, which generally lasts until the next time they are disturbed. Then there are people who feel like they are suffocating in the comfort zone. As soon as they reach a milestone or reach one goal, they look for adventure, opportunity, and are always looking for more. They lead their lives and live to the best of their abilities. The first group of people is taking the passenger seat and the second group acts as drivers. They make their destiny and live life as they imagine before their time is up.

The most important thing in your life is your time on this earth. This is the time that you are alive and breathing. This time is very short. When you are in your teenage years, forty years sounds a long time, but when are in your forties, sit and wonder how time slipped away so fast. This is why I feel it is very important for you to read this book to learn how to make the right decision based on your own values and dreams so you don't have any regrets at the end of your limited lifetime.

Life is half science and half art. We all have the science part of it down, but only a few can get the art part of life. We have all the technical skills, but don't have the quality of life we deserve. We are taught about all kinds of different subjects, but not the art of dealing with ups and downs in the cycles of life. We learn how to read and use the clock when we are in first or second grade, and we can fill up every minute of our life with "to-do" lists. However, do you carry a map and a compass with you to navigate your way through life? This book can become a guide to empower you to live a happy, sexy and rich life.

What are the 7 Treasures You Own?

The seven treasures are your own natural treasure chests. They are all yours already. All you need to do is add to them as much as possible so you have a reservoir when you need to withdraw from them. They are your health, feelings, knowledge, faith, family, career, and wealth. Just like a real treasure chest, if you deposit into them, you can withdraw from them when you are in need or when you want to. For instance, when you exercise and energize your body you are adding and depositing into this treasure, and then when you are sick you can start using from your reserve of stored energy and power. When you read a book, you deposit something into the treasure of your intelligence so that when you need it, you can withdraw this knowledge and use it.

The first and most important treasure is your health. It is your body, because if you don't have your body, or if you have a body with disease, you will lose all other treasures that you have. Your good health and energetic body will carry you today and every day for many years. You are supposed to have eyes to see the beauty; you are supposed to have ears to listen to the music that is playing only for you; you are supposed to have the limbs to move, to touch, to create, and to help you live comfortably. Yet I don't know why we abuse our health and ignore signs of pain and discomfort. After all, we are mostly made of bones and muscles which work autonomously to help us breath and be alive. Our body needs a set of requirements in order to work at an optimal level. Our health is our most valued treasure and we should learn ways to add value to it if we want to live for a long time.

Your second asset or treasure is your feelings. You are giving this inner power system which, besides your physical attributes, introduces you to the world. People will know and remember you based on your emotions. For instance, 'so and so' is very happy, positive, kind, brave, nice, jealous, sad, negative... You get the idea. How you are perceived as a person depends heavily on your upbringing and how your parents raised you. However, if you had less than an ideal childhood, you can never blame them for the things that have gone wrong in your life. The moment you know yourself and become responsible for your own decisions, you have a chance to make your own personality and introduce it to the world. The famous and the most successful people in the world have been those with positive, happy, kind, and brave attitudes. So, it must be good. To start your own positive change, catch yourself with negative, sad, and bad feelings, and change it right away to see the positive and happy side of your situation at that moment. By doing this, you just added something to your emotional treasure, and you will feel good about it right away.

Third, you have the treasure of your knowledge and wisdom. This treasure is empty when you are born. You add something new to it every day. The most critical time of adding and depositing into your brain is when you are growing up. Your first teachers were your parents, and then your school teachers. Frank Tibolt, in *Touch of Greatness* states that "We have 12 billion brain cells, and we only use a small fraction of it." William James and other great psychologists tell us: "Compared to what we should be, we are only half awake. We are making use of only a small part of our mind. Deep down inside us are powers we know nothing of and never use." In this case, we have the capacity to add to this asset all the time to improve our thinking, knowledge, and wisdom, in order to be able to make better decisions in our everyday life matters.

The fourth treasure is your spiritual being. You have this asset that you cannot see or hear. You can only feel it. However, most of the time, it whispers the rights and wrongs of your actions to your ears. Some people might call this consciousness. Whatever you call it, it must stand for something. For many, it is their religion or certain activities that help them connect to the larger universe. They find answers for their problems and thank the Creator for their blessings. In the big picture of this universe, every one of us needs to find out where we came from and where we are going. This treasure acts as a compass that guides us to the good and stops us from the bad. We do need to take the time to find ourselves, our guidance, and our connection to the universe. Your quiet time, prayer time, and meditation time to be with yourself and your Creator, adds to this treasure daily.

The fifth treasure is your family. Ultimately, you are a social being and you need other human beings to share your good and bad moments with. All of you depend on your parents and family at first, but then you expand and connect to people you meet. You know their strengths and weaknesses; you reach out to help them, hoping that they will do the same for you. So, in essence, everyone you meet can be in your family asset and you can be in someone else's. When you reach out and help someone without any immediate reward then you have added something to your family treasure. You will be rewarded one day when you need it.

The sixth treasure is your career. You do need to do something for a living - something that is according to your strengths and passion. If what you do is not according to your passion, you are in the wrong occupation. Your health, emotions, wisdom, faith, family and wealth depend on your career. Thus, it is very important to choose the right career because you spend half of your life doing it. When you go to school to advance your career or to start a new career, you make a deposit into this treasure that you can use at any time you want to in the future.

Seventh, and the least important but the most sought after treasure, is your wealth or financial treasure. Everyone has some kind of money coming and going regularly. Do you want more money coming? Then, the best way to earn more money is to do this: keep yourself healthy, have a positive attitude, learn more, have faith, treasure your family, and use your own passion. I bet that if you put your attention into the six treasures above, your seventh treasure will be full and you won't even know how you did it. Of course there is a need to learn, and it does require daily practice not only on income and expenses, but also on how to keep most of the money you have earned.

How to Make Decisions with 7 Treasures?

As soon as you open your eyes in the morning you ought to make decisions – small or large. Sometimes you are in bed when you decide to call in sick to work. Sometimes you still haven't opened your eyes yet when you decide to hire or fire someone from their job today. You are still in the shower when you decide to have cereal for breakfast or skip coffee or whether to wear that green jacket today. You are always faced with the guilt and responsibility of making the wrong decisions, some of which could be very costly to your well-being, your stress, your body, your family, your career and your wealth.

Using the 7 treasures method and following it with every decision, you can be sure that you will not regret your actions because you make decisions consciously and based on principle. Your best decisions are then based on your own values and goals. **First, when you are faced with an action to make a decision, see if it adds value to one or more of your treasures. If yes,**

say, "Yes," and do it immediately. If the answer is no, refuse to do it and stand firm on your decision. If you feel like you are withdrawing you have to make sure that it is not for a long time, as you will run out of resources and need to refill your treasures - for instance, when you want to call in sick to work, you are withdrawing from several of your treasures, such as your wealth and your career, but perhaps you decided to spend the day with family and are thus depositing into your family, health, and feelings treasures. Depending on what makes you happy at the moment and which one of your treasures is an important priority to you, you can call in sick and spend the day with your family.

Very shortly you will know how to keep the balance in adding and withdrawing from your treasures. If one or two of your 7 treasures are weaker than the rest, you need to pay more attention and try to add more value to your weaknesses. Let me remind you about one thing: everything you do during your 24 hours fits into your 7 treasures. Therefore, you can very easily remind yourself to use this fact when making decisions. You will know that you made your decision based on your values and wishes. You can then take responsibility for your decision and will not have any regrets later.

Let me share this true story with you on how successful people make up their mind fast. Oliver Napoleon Hill was born to a poor family in 1883. He fought his way out of his backwoods Virginia town with a burning desire to be successful. He was always searching for ways to improve himself and was involved in numerous ventures, including managing a coalmine, practicing law, and becoming a business journalist. His big break came when he had the opportunity of meeting Andrew Carnegie, the "Steel King." Andrew Carnegie asked Napoleon Hill if he would take up the challenge of devoting 20 years of his life, in order to prepare a formula of success for helping others to become successful. Andrew Carnegie would provide him with letters of reference to meet hundreds of successful people, such as Woodrow Wilson, Henry Ford, Thomas Edison, Theodore Roosevelt, John D. Rockefeller, to name a few. Napoleon Hill made his decision to take up the challenge in less than 60 seconds. Later he came to know that Andrew Carnegie had given him 60 seconds to make up his mind, failing which he would have lost his chance of undertaking the important assignment. After 20 years of dedicated research in 1937, he came out with his best seller, "Think And Grow Rich," which has helped countless people around the world to achieve success. One of his famous sayings was, "Whatever the mind of man can conceive and believe it can achieve."

Keeping the best interests of your 7 Treasures in mind, you make a conscious choice and concrete decision based on your knowledge, values, and reasons. You will live in peace knowing that you can take responsibility for your bad decisions and make them correct the moment you realize they are wrong.

Mistakes are inevitable in life, and you should welcome mistakes as a stepping-stone to your next chapter of life. So never be afraid of making decisions – even if it is not a good one.

How to Start Using the 7 Treasures?

Simple; you can start by where you are and what you are doing now. It is very normal to lose sight and always be on the driving force for upward mobility. Only occasionally do we find ourselves stopping to appreciate the things that we already have. These can be our good health, good friends, family, and many other personal things. Benjamin Jowett, an English Scholar, has said that "the real measure of your wealth is how much you would be worth if you lost all your money." There are ups and downs in everybody's life. This is a fact of life that you have to accept. When times are good, we tend to feel proud and full of ourselves. However, when times are bad, we tend to get depressed and blame something else for our failure. This is the exact cycle that prevents you from enjoying life and enjoying what you already have. Once you accept that you are doing your best under all circumstances, nothing happens to you unexpectedly to make you feel like a failure. You can be prepared for all unexpected situations; deal with them one at a time, and accept that life is a flowing trend of ups and downs.

All of us have projects and things to do before we think we should start to live our dream life. Let me share this story with you on life with no worries. One day a young man went to see a wise man about his life. As he sat down with the wise man, he started pouring out all his problems and challenges in life. He said that he was indeed unfortunate and asked the wise man for advice. The wise man smiled. He then handed to the young man a small slip of paper with an address written on it. The wise man said, "When you find this place, where all the residents there have no problems, challenges, or worries, you can then ask them for their advice." The young man was excited and started looking for the place. After a long search, he found the place. It was a cemetery!

And then there are others who are affected by events around them. They become pessimistic and lose hope by watching their local news. They wonder how we can enjoy our lives when everything goes wrong around us. I have to say that the solution to that is to make one change, if they can, to make one wrong step right, and then feel good about it. We are born to be happy and content, and the only person taking happiness from our life is ourselves. No one has the power to make us unhappy. So, taking responsibility for our own happiness is the key to enjoying life at all moments.

You might say that I am very selfish to want to be happy at all times, or that I do not feel other people's pain – hunger, war, disease, rivalry, bad relationships, troubled kids, demanding parents, or stressful jobs. I have to say that I cannot ignore the pain, suffering, and injustice of the world, but I do as much as I can in order to have a satisfied conscious. If you think you can make a difference in the world, even if it is by doing the smallest thing, I suggest you do it if you are capable. However, I feel that we have responsibility for our own life first and foremost. Someone once said, "The only way to help the poor is not to be poor yourself." When you take care of yourself and get rid of all your pain, the world will have one less suffering person.

To assure myself that I am not going to be able to solve all the suffering in the world, I am hanging Reinhold Niebuhr's "Serenity Prayer" on my wall: "God grant me the serenity to accept the things I cannot change; courage to change the things I can; and wisdom to know the difference."

How to Value Your Time?

There is only one thing in your life that is scarce, and that is your time. Think about the richest person in the world, and think about how long he or she lived. Now think about a person that has been born to be poor and struggling all of his or her life. Why would the poor person be alive, if the length of your life depended on money, belongings, or status? All of us open our eyes one day; live a number of days, and then that is it. We all have to leave one day. As I mentioned before, when we are twenty-something, we look at forty-year-olds as if they are too old, but when we get there, forty does not seem like that long. Life passes us by very fast if we drive through it in a rush.

Everything else besides time is endless, and you might not get to the end of it all before your time runs out. For this reason, make sure that how you spend your time and your day-to-day activities fills your life with things you love and that make you happy and deposits into your 7 treasures. Knowing how your decisions affect your life, you will look at and do things differently to get yourself closer to a balanced and happy life. You will then not regret anything when you are old and at the end of your rope.

Most believe that they come into this world at a certain time, and will leave this world at a pre-defined time, as is intended by the Creator. The universe seems to work in a most accurate way that is still an unknown mystery. The sad part is that we don't know when our time will be up. It might be years from now or it might be tomorrow.

For this reason, every breath that we are taking makes us one breath closer to the end of our time. This is a reality for which no one personally takes time to evaluate their existence and answer very important questions about their lives. When we are young in middle school and high school we might have thought about what we were going to be when we were grown up, but that thought vanished once we reached into adulthood. We always feel that obstacles do not let us get to our goals and dreams. There is always someone or something that prevents us from reaching our desired life.

How Can You Live In The Present?

Most of the inspirational leaders' advice is to live in the moment. However, practicing it actually is very difficult. You can very easily forget to live in the present. One thing or another occupies your mind and you lose sight of this moment. It takes practice and daily reminders to stay in the present moment without rushing, worrying, or dwelling on regrets of the past.

Past events or future occurrences are not relevant to how you should live the present moment. Where you are at the present moment is a result of your past decisions. If you like where you are, this is good, but if you don't like it, now is the time to change it. You can only learn from what has happened in past mistakes, and you can certainly make your future better with the good decisions you make in the present moment.

In order to reach your goals and make your dreams come true, mind your own 7 Treasures and spend all your time depositing into them. This book will make it easy for you to deal with your day-to-day challenges and make your best decisions based on the rules of the

7 Treasures. Remember that my goal is to make your life as easy, happy, and as rewarding as possible. My aim is not for you to memorize or follow some strict rule. Life happens every minute and no one can be aware of his or her next minute.

Work Sheets & Daily 7 Reminders:

At the end of each chapter is a worksheet that will focus your attention on what is most important in your life. You will know your priorities and know how to make tough decisions in a split second.

Please fill out the worksheets thoroughly and thoughtfully, as all the questions help you understand your hidden treasures. With daily reminder lists, you will have something to work with every day. Practice and you will reach to your potential for a happy and balanced life.

PREPETORY WORKSHEET:

What are your regrets in life now?

_____

_____

_____

What can you do about them now?

_____

_____

_____

Give a reason to forgive yourself for your regrets and
move on?

_____

_____

_____

Give a reason to forgive others for your regrets and
move on?

_____

_____

_____

What is your ideal life? (Describe it in detail)

_____

_____

_____

What are your favorite activities?

_____

_____

_____

What makes you happy?

_____

_____

_____

What can you do to get yourself closer to your ideal life?

_____

_____

_____

Exercise:

Visit a cemetery close to your home. I know that this is not an ideal thing to do for many, but sooner or later, we are all going to be there. When reading the head stones, reflect on the following:

1. What would they have been doing now if they were not dead?

2. What would happen if you were in their place?

"The greatest wealth is health."

Virgil

1st:

Treasure of Health:

There is a thousand-year-old Persian phrase that says, "The world is alive because I am alive." We can see, feel, and do things when we are alive. Nothing makes a difference for a person who lies beneath the earth or is no longer breathing. So, our breath is our life and it is the most important thing that we have. We have to do everything possible to make sure we breathe for as long as possible.

It is also a Persian phrase that says, "With good health, you are the King," meaning that even if you don't have anything but you are in good health, you should consider yourself a "King." And vice versa if a King is sick he is considered a poor man, as despite having everything, cannot enjoy anything.

I have asked many elderly people to give me their best advice for a young person on how to live life. Almost every single one has said, "To *know the value of your time and go for the things that you want to accomplish*." This is really good advice, but the big question is how to include this thought in our daily life.

I have already talked about valuing your time, and you are aware that there is only one of you in this world with a pre-defined time on this earth. You don't have time to waste if you are a person with dreams, goals, and ambition. I am sure that everyone, like me, has a list of things to do, places to see, and events to experience. However, you are undoubtedly not going to get there if you don't have a well and able body – your health.

Our goal is survival and living longer, and this depends on our body and good health. Thus, our health is an asset that we are given. All we have to do is add value to it constantly so we can last long and function over a long time.

Aside from people who are born with a health issue, most people are capable of taking care of their body and having optimal health. As we are part of the nature that we are living in, we should naturally live with good health. However, there are many elements that cause disease. Our only weapon against these elements is to be prepared for them and fight them.

Very briefly I will go over the most important things that make our bodies strong. Of course, you can find detailed information on how to take care of your health and body online and in bookstores. My aim here is to outline the most important things that you can remember from the start to the end of your day. Our body, or health treasure, needs us to add **healthy foods**, **exercise**, and **sleep**, on a daily basis.

HEALTHY FOOD:

As far as food goes, it is very good to remember the fact that anything that goes into your mouth starts at the time of grocery shopping. All food that you eat is either deposited into your body and gives you positive energy, or withdrawn and gives you negative energy. Now it is your decision to understand balance and differentiate between good food and bad food. You need to know how much energy you need to intake in 24 hours. If you are very active and physical, you need more energy than someone who is not. Evaluate your level of activity during the day and adjust the balance of your food intake. You should avoid impulsive or emotion-based eating. Sometimes we eat food just because we feel like it based on stress, happiness or sadness, which is wrong.

You also have to evaluate your relationship with food as it relates to you culturally. Afghanistan, where I grew up, is a very poor country. Food is scarce for many, and the majority of the population work very hard to provide some kind of food for their family. Many do not have a choice of what to eat, but rather eat whatever they can afford to buy on that day. I remember that a good meal consisted of high animal protein and lots of oil. However, here in America food is not scarce. Even the poor here have an abundance of choice when they go to the supermarkets to buy food. It is also important to consider how significant food was in your family when you were a child. Did your family have healthy eating habits? Were you eating home cooked meals or prepared and processed food? Were you eating together with everyone around or eating individually on everyone's own timeframe?

It is very important to look at food as being plentiful, and to feel that you have choices of what to eat. You don't need too many kinds of food on your table for every meal to be satisfied, but rather you only need to have a little of each food group to keep yourself going. Eating small portions more frequently will keep your energy level the same throughout the day. Eating more for breakfast and less for dinner is recommended for a good metabolism rate, as well as a getting good night's sleep and maintaining a normal weight.

Keep this chart handy and follow the recommended servings:

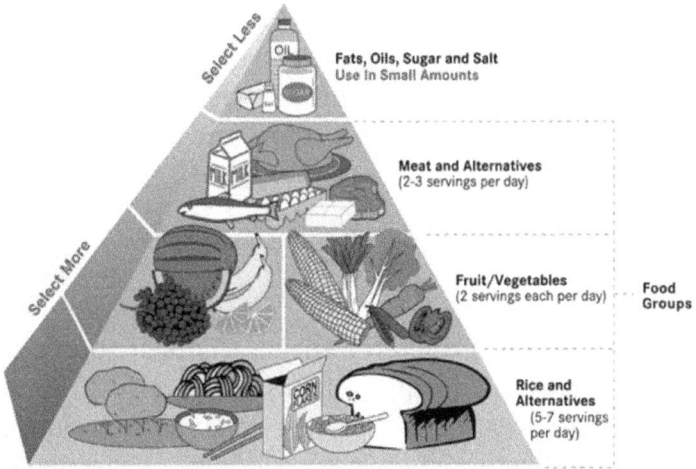

Carbohydrates:

Having small portions of foods rich in carbohydrates throughout the day is very important for providing the fuel needed to break down protein and enzymes that you need for your metabolism. This is also a very complex food group to understand. Good carbohydrates come from whole grain bread, brown rice, whole grain pasta, potatoes, whole grain cereal, and beans.

Fruits and Vegetables:

This is another necessary food group that you should have at least two to three servings per day, but in small portions. Fruits and vegetables give you vitamins and minerals that your body needs. The best thing is to eat a variety of them in different colors and always choose the ripest ones.

Protein:

You need to eat protein for energy. A major source of protein comes from animals. However, it is recommended to eat as little animal protein as possible and get most of your protein from alternative sources. And when you eat meat, you should stay away from large (complex) animals and choose small (simple) animals. The smallest animals, at the bottom of the food chain, are healthier than large animals. Fish is a very good source of protein and omega 3 oils. It is recommended to eat fish as much as three to four times a week. Alternatives to animal protein are legumes, grains, vegetables, fruits, and nuts and seeds that are rich in protein.

Legumes: Garbanzo beans, kidney beans, lentils, lima beans, soy beans, and split peas.

Grains: Barley, brown rice, buckwheat, millet, oatmeal, quinoa, rye, wheat germ, wheat, and wild rice.

Vegetables: Artichokes, beets, broccoli, Brussels sprouts, cabbage, cauliflower, cucumbers, eggplant, green peas, green pepper, kale, lettuce, mushroom, mustard green, onions, potatoes, spinach, tomatoes, turnip greens, watercress, yams, and zucchini.

Fruits: Apple, banana, cantaloupe, grape, grapefruit, honeydew melon, orange, papaya, peach, pear, pineapple, strawberry, tangerine, and watermelon.

Nuts & Seeds: Almonds, cashews, filberts, hemp seeds, peanuts, pumpkin seeds, sesame seeds, sunflower seeds, and walnuts.

Fats/Sweets and Salts:

This group should be used as little as possible. The best kinds of oils are olive, grape seeds, canola and vegetable oils. All types of animal fats and oils should be avoided. An alternative to sugar is honey, and alternative to salt can be spices like sumac to flavor your food.

Liquids:

According to many sources I have discovered, our body is made up of up to 60% water. Keeping our body hydrated is very important. You can prevent sickness and diseases by drinking plenty of water. I have read that water can be used for headaches, joint pains (arthritis), clearing skin, and healthy hair. Usually, drinking room temperature water before meals is recommended.

Spices and Sauces:

Spices are important since they are natural remedies of the ancients. They are used to give flavor, texture, or color to your food. Spices are natural enhancers and have many health benefits.

Miracle Food:

There is a group of foods that I have to mention here that act as miracle foods. They are known for longevity, good health, and preventing diseases. These are: onions, garlic, ginger, lemon, dates, figs, and honey.

Vitamin Supplements:

It is possible to get all your necessary vitamins and minerals from the food that you are eating. However, if you feel that your eating habits are not optimal or that you are too busy to pay attention to your food regimen, it is best to take the necessary supplements. However, you have to be very careful and choose the best kind from a well-known company. To be safe with your health, it is important to take supplements under the guidance of a physician.

Foods to Avoid:

Canned food, processed food, sodas, snack bars, alcohol, pastry, and fried food.

SLEEP / REST:

You have to think of your body as an automatic machine that is on 24-7. This natural machine also needs time to refresh and repair after periods of constant activity. Your energy and cycles of your systems are refreshed after each night's sleep. This is why it is important to have a good night's sleep in order to feel rejuvenated every morning.

Babies and sick people need more sleep because their bodies need to grow or restore back to an optimal level of health and energy.

If at all possible, if you have the luxury of putting a few minutes aside during the day, you must take it. Quick power naps magically restore energy. It is like putting two days of work into one day. Some companies in Japan require their employees to take naps in the middle of the day to prevent fatigue and increase production. You have to make sure that these naps are not close to the evening, as it will prevent you from your normal sleeping time at night.

How much sleep is enough? My search shows that it really depends on each person and their level of physical activity. A highly active person needs more time for sleep to rejuvenate and restore than a person who undertakes less physical activity. The amount of sleep also depends on the habits of the individual. An active person, who cannot spend more hours in bed, trains the body to get enough rest at a shorter amount of time – 6 hours instead of 8. What is important is that you train your body to regularly sleep at a certain time and wake up at a certain time. For some reason when that cycle breaks, the body feels pressure and fatigue until you give it enough time to get back to normal again.

The quality of sleep and nap is much more important than its length of time. Sometimes five minutes of deep sleep is more effective than twenty minutes of superficial nap.

Fighting Sleeplessness:

You have to realize that a normal body in optimal health will fall asleep very comfortably after you slip into your bed. If you are awake and cannot fall asleep, something is not working well in your body or you are stressing over something that cannot leave your thoughts. This is a serious issue that you should not let go on for a long time, as it could damage a part of you permanently. I will share more about some of the things that have helped me fall asleep quickly, and then sleep like a baby all night.

Comfortable bed and temperature: this is something that is within your control. If you think that you are spending half of your life on your bed, then you must pay a little more attention to the quality of your mattress, the most comfortable pillow, and the most cuddling comforter. The sleeping atmosphere and temperature is all personal and based on your individuality. Some like it dark, some like it colder, some hot, and some can sleep with the light on. It is a priceless investment for you to find your comfort level for a good night's sleep.

Exercise/activity: If you can remember the days that you were most active, you most likely fell asleep really fast and deeply too. When you take your children to the park and have them run around and expend a lot of energy, they fall asleep fast and stay asleep for a long time. These are clues to understand. If and when you don't have enough activity during the day, your body doesn't feel like restoring because it has not expended any energy. Just do some exercise during the day to have a long and good night's sleep.

The best solution I have found, if a problem is keeping me awake at night, is to leave it for tomorrow when I wake up. I usually have faith that some larger power than myself will handle it for me, and everything will magically be solved. Believe it or not, more often than not this becomes true. So, I have found that I will never solve a problem by stressing over it while I want to go to sleep. This has become the best way to overcome the nighttime worries obstacle.

Other things that I have tried are praying to clear my mind from un-necessary stresses. Through prayer, I find myself vulnerable to all those events that are out of my control. I reassure myself that if I live one more day, the Almighty will take care of everything for me.

Other things I do include checking for all those annoying sounds of dripping water, open doors and windows, and whatever else there might be. I have also tried reading, which has worked really well for me.

Again it all depends on your person and your comfort level. The most important part is that you take it seriously, and have a long and deep sleep so you can begin each new day with new and fresh energy.

PHYSICAL EXERCISE:

After eating food and sleeping as you usually do, you need to have some kind of physical activity during the day. This is as important as food and rest for keeping your body at an optimal balance, both in appearance and internally. Exercise strengthens all of your body: bones, blood stream, breathing, heart, digestion, and brain. It prevents your body from storing fat and gaining weight, as well as calming the nerves and de-stressing the mind. It works as a medicine for fatigue and depression.

Doctors recommend at least half an hour of continuous and fast movement. This causes the heart to pump blood faster throughout your body and improves the circulation. Of course there are many different ways to do this. You have to find your own personal favorite activity so you enjoy it as well. The list of possible exercises is very long and it can include walking, biking, jogging, swimming, dancing, boxing, or kickboxing.

Your body is made of many systems, and millions and millions of cells. If you viewed your cells under a microscope, you could see your cells moving. They are alive and have energy that makes up your body. I read in a book once that all of your cells are in constant movement and constantly change. They grow, split, change shape, and die off to the point that every three years you get all new cells in your body.

Your body cells are alive, creating energy and producing waste. The waste is given to the blood stream to be taken out of your body. This is where fast and rapid pumping of your blood stream takes toxins and waste out of your body through perspiration. Drinking water while exercising helps to take out more toxins. As a result, fresh and new cells keep your organs and your body healthy and young.

Keeping a balance in your exercise activities is the key. You cannot overdo any of the workouts because it can cause extra burden on your joints and bones. You just have to remember that doing too much of the good things can hurt you instead of help you. The key is to have balance and steady progress by slowly building more exercise time, frequency, and endurance.

Aerobics:

To get oxygen to the trillions cells of your body, improve your circulation, heart, lungs, and all the systems of your body, you need to have your heart work hard for a short time several days per week. Doing so gives you more energy and good feelings. This activity gets all of the dangerous toxins out of your body. You just have to find your favorite activity, or alternate to keep variety, and stay motivated. You can choose to go to the gym and spend some time on the machines, or do open exercises like running, jogging, swimming, ball playing, jump rope, and dancing. Health practitioners recommend at least half an hour of aerobics three to four times a week.

Weight Training:

Weight training is very important for building muscles. You need strong and healthy muscles to protect your bones and help you with every day activities. The best time to do weight training is after aerobic exercise when the body and muscles are warm. You can use dumbbells, rubber bands, or weight training machines. It is important to start slow with small weights and gradually increase. Slow, steady and controlled movement is most effective. Each session should be in three sets of eight to ten repetitions. The weight needs to be adjusted and set to challenge muscle endurance – not too easy or too hard. The best way to lift a heavy weight and work out a muscle is to take a deep breath in on the way up and steadily release the weight with your exhale out under smooth control. You'll see how easy it will be to go one step further with each breath. Overall, balance and steady work are the main points that make your activities efficient.

Stretching:

After aerobic and weight training, it is time to stretch for flexibility. After you pump oxygen into your muscles and work them hard with weights, you will want to calm them down with stretching. These are free movements in any way or shape that you want to bend and extend your body parts. Yoga is an excellent way to do this. This part of your exercise routine helps improve attitude and promotes good feelings.

APPEARANCE:

The first impression of your body is very important. If you do everything above with eating right, sleeping well, and exercising regularly, you are sure to have a good physical appearance. In addition to the above, you need to pay close attention to your hygiene as well. Skin, hair, nails, and teeth shape your character and personality. Whatever you may be inside, if your outside does not represent that, no one will know you. Just imagine when you see a car mechanic wearing a uniform, a taxi driver, a chef, a professor, a businessman, or a doctor.... You will probably guess what they do the first time you see them. This is why it is important to look exactly like the one person for whom you want to be known.

If you are someone who naturally has good skin, you are one of the lucky ones. For the ones who need a little help in this area, it is worth investing some time, energy, and money to look as good as possible. Of course, if you are eating right, sleeping well, drinking a lot of water, and are exercising, you will naturally have clear skin. If extra help is needed, it is worth it to get some products that help clear the skin, especially for your face, neck and hands.

Groomed hair with clean and clipped nails can very well represent your personality. Pay extra attention to having clean teeth, mouth and body odors. Healthy skin, hair, teeth, and nails, are the first things that other people notice on you. They represent you as a healthy and rich person no matter how wealthy you are with your bank account. It is possible for anyone to accomplish this.

Looking good also depends on your style of clothing and footwear. Your clothes must represent you. If you like to be serious and professional, your wardrobe should be full of serious and professional clothes like jackets, collared shirts, suites. Professional clothes take the attention off your body, and place it on your objective and your words. You have to find out the right clothing for the right occasion. You have to pay attention to wear the right clothing for your character. Therefore, make sure to have eveningwear, sportswear, and casual clothing in your closet. You don't have to spend a fortune on your clothes, but spend your money wisely. You can use discount stores, thrift stores, and seasonal sales to buy quality clothing.

More than anything else, your shoes tell who you are. You can walk with confidence when you wear comfortable shoes. You would be surprised to know the effects of uncomfortable shoes on your day. First of all, they can hurt your legs and your body; they can damage your posture and your back; they can stress you out at a very important moment in your day. This is especially important for women as some women force their feet into very high heels, and uncomfortable but pretty shoes. You can test yourself with different shoes and see how they make you feel. Follow your body as a guide to what kind of shoes you need to wear.

Doing your tasks without hurry and at your own body's pace is healthy. Rushing is withdrawing from your body's treasure as your heart works faster than it is supposed to do against your body's natural pace. You make more mistakes and waste energy. You can feel too tired and exhausted to enjoy the rest of the day.

In general, your body needs sunlight and fresh air. You can breathe cleaner air and get much needed oxygen and vitamin D for your skin and other organs. A few deep, slow, and steady breaths can help you in many ways and be deposited into your physical treasure chest. Light can reduce depression and bring energy.

1st – Treasure of Health – Work Sheet:

I will add the following protein to my diet:

_____

_____

_____

I will shop for the following vegetables this week:

_____

_____

_____

I will eliminate the following unhealthy food from my
diet:

_____

_____

_____

I will pay attention to these aches and pains in my
body:

_____

_____

_____

I will do the following to alleviate my pain today:

_____

_____

_____

I will do the following activities to sleep better:

_____

_____

_____

I will do these physical activities this week:

_____

_____

_____

I will do the following improvements to my appearance:

_____

_____

_____

1st – Treasure of Health: 7 Daily Reminders:

1. Acknowledge your breath the moment you wake up and look forward to another beautiful day.

2. Decide on the spot if the food you are about to put in your mouth adds to your good health or withdraws from your good health – whether to eat it or not.

3. Eat a variety of colorful food more frequently in small portions. More vegetables, fruits, white meat and seafood should make up the majority of your food intake.

4. Drink 8-10 cups of water daily.

5. Mandate yourself half an hour of physical activity every day. Soon it will become a habit that you can't live without. Exercise for more energy, good sleep, good posture, and a healthy body.

6. Dress to impress – your healthy, clean, and beautiful body.

7. Remember that there is only one of you in the world, and your time is limited. Live one day at a time.

"Without feelings of respect, what is there
to distinguish men from beasts?"

Confucius

2nd:

Treasure of Feelings:

After the first impression of our body and good health, we are known for what is inside: our feelings, personality and character. Our conversation says a lot about who we really are. Meeting someone with a good and positive personality is always memorable. We enjoy spending time with that person, learn from that person, and the doors to further friendship open from this first meeting.

Almost everybody knows what good and bad traits of a person are. We have heard it from our parents, teachers, friends, family members, and acquaintances. I believe that there is good in every bad person and there is bad in every good person. Whether we are good or bad all depends on the situation and the mood. We don't necessarily choose to have bad behaviors, but sometimes we just don't know a better way to express our thoughts. We usually make a quick judgment of the other person and the atmosphere before we show our good or bad side. Sometimes our conversations depend on how we feel at the moment. In situations where we are comfortable, we are able to share our true feelings. However, in situations where we are threatened, we often try to hide our feelings and pretend to be someone else.

Our parents are the first teachers of our personality, but I do believe that there is more to it. Some of us have a genetic connection to our behavior. My mother told me that I wasn't crying when I was a newborn and she had to wake me up to feed me. My quietness really bothers her to this day, and I think this is how I was born. Some people could have medical reasons for their behavior or other sources outside of their family and normal life. However, our parents were the first people to let us know if we did something good or bad in our early ages. We did our best to gain their approval and attention in whatever we did. This attitude remains with us all of our lives. We feel the need to have somebody's approval for our actions and behaviors, whether it is our parents, family or friends. Many of us have learned to hide our true selves and true feelings because we are looking for approval. We are afraid that others might not approve or that we might hurt our loved ones. This is the main reason why people try very hard to fit in and be normal enough in their immediate circle of influence.

Many psychology studies show that people who value their own feelings and don't need to do something for other people's satisfaction or approval, live happier lives. We feel most happy when we express our inner wants and desires. We appreciate more, see beauty in small places, and look for good in others; we have patience, take responsibility for our own actions and decisions, and shape our own destiny, where we live a happy and balanced life.

However, somewhere along the way, we lose track and find it difficult to express our true feelings. For instance, we fail to say, "I love you," to the people we really love. We don't thank enough; we talk more than we should; we feel our problems and projects are more important than others; we make demands, criticize, and get upset easily. We become a mean or unfriendly person.

To go back to our normal state of being free and happy, the first step is to differentiate and acknowledge positive and negative situations in our lives. Then, we need to unwind many things that we have learned throughout the years. We should consciously work on expressing our feelings and training ourselves to deposit into the treasure of our feelings with the following actions.

Love Yourself:

Love and respect yourself as much as you want others to love and respect you. This way others, even your parents and siblings, notice your feelings and emotions and value your character. When the closest people to you know that you take your emotions and your feelings serious, they try to respect them and spread what is important to you to your larger circle of influence. If you don't respect and value your own feelings, no one else will.

Leave Your Childhood Emotions Behind:

There are many things that happen in your childhood that are sad or bad experiences. Abused as a child, bullied in school, suffered a loss, didn't have kind and nurturing family, and lack of attachment, could all be forgiven. As you grow older and take charge of your own life, it is time to get rid of unhappy experiences and create new memories for your future. Sad childhood experiences have already shaped your personality and you can use those experiences as good lessons to achieve bigger and better accomplishments. Any time you realize that your childhood memories are holding you back, making you vulnerable and debilitating you, that is the time to forgive and move on.

Take Responsibility / No Blame Game:

No one wins when you blame someone else or some other situation for your life situations. Our parents raised us the best way they knew how. Now as a responsible adult, you can make decisions and reach your goals. If you have failed in something or something bad has happened to you, it is only because you were vulnerable, oblivious, or were not prepared to stop it. Your failures and past misfortunes can serve as most valuable lessons in your life, making you stronger and better prepared for future.

You Reap What You Sow:

This is an old metaphor that makes a lot of sense. Whatever you plant in your garden, you expect to get that. If you are planting hate, you sow hate. If you plant kindness, you get kindness. Some of us have expectations from others that might be unrealistic. When things don't go your way, you simply have to take responsibility and know that it was your actions that brought the current situation upon you. This is in normal long term content of a balanced life. I am not referring to accidents or violent acts upon you on a short term basis.

Positive Thinking and Optimism:

One of the most important attributes that helps you carry on and look toward a better future is positive thinking and being optimistic. I truly believe that some people are born with this habit and some people need to learn it throughout their lives. And, there are some people who are just born to be negative and see the ugly and sad side of every issue and every person. Most of the time people are negative because they are trying to protect themselves or defend their actions. Or, perhaps they haven't forgiven and forgotten their bad memories. Negative thinkers always look at things that have happened and blame others for their miseries. It is possible to learn to be positive, and look at the bright and good side of things and people. Another option is to consciously take a minute and analyze what are your complaints, and change your perspective about them. For example, I did not want to manage a fast food restaurant and work seven days a week, but at the time I had no other choice but to change my perspective about it. I looked at my day as feeding many hungry customers, and then I felt differently about my job. This perspective kept me going with my restaurant for eight years.

A man was playing catch with his dog on a beach. He proudly shouted to his friend, showing off what his dog was doing. He threw the ball really high and far into the water, and his dog ran into the water to catch the ball. The man was expecting that his friend would be impressed by his dog's action, but the friend said, "Oh, your dog cannot swim." The friend did not see the extraordinary running ability of the dog but instead pointed out something negative about the situation. This is a good exercise for you to catch yourself in different situations if you see anything negative about something. In this case, deliberately look for something positive to note as well. You will eventually make a habit of looking at positives in the future.

Positive thinkers are creators and producers of new ideas, possibilities, and opportunities. They go over any obstacles that are in their way and get themselves to their goal. If you know one, you might agree with me that they are happier and healthier, with at least some degree of success in their social and financial life.

Gratitude:

One trait that gets you closer to positive thinking is gratitude: the ability to be thankful for every situation and every person that encounters you. The first gratitude should come out from your Creator giving you this life with all its beauty in it. There are many things that you can be thankful for having. Your good health, your family, your friends, or your good spirits, your good looks, and your skills, are each gifts that should be thankful for.

Helping Others and Volunteering:

Helping is the ultimate contributor of happiness and feeling good. To be needed and to be able to fulfill a need is a happy feeling. When you solve a problem, take care a sick person, help out a family member in need, volunteer at your community and see a smile in another person's face, it all brings you better and higher contentment.

Anthony Robbins, the famous author and motivational speaker, told of a story of giving from when he was a kid. When he was young, his parents worked extremely hard to take care of the family. On one Thanksgiving night when the family had nothing to eat, the doorbell rang and someone delivered a box full of food and turkey for them. They were told it was from someone who loved and cared about them and did not want anything in return. Anthony never forgot this experience, so every Thanksgiving he buys a week's worth of grocery and turkey and delivers it to a needy family without disclosing himself. He leaves a note behind saying, "This is from someone who cares about you with the hopes someday you will take good care of yourself and return this favor to someone else in need."

Do you remember other people's acts of kindness, or better yet, have you ever thought about returning a favor to someone else in need?

Saving Money:

Usually when you are concentrating on making ends meet, you become inward and unfriendly. You feel hopeless and helpless. One way to get yourself out of this situation is to spend as little as possible for a while so you can regularly save some money. Remember that living with as much as you can afford or paycheck to paycheck will always keep you poor. Having some money on the side always adds to your peace of mind and you don't feel hopeless or helpless any more.

Time Alone and Time with Friends:

I know that it is not easy to allocate some time for yourself alone, but it is possible if you make it a priority. It is much rewarding to have time to shop, read, and write, to have a cup of coffee and to relax or do anything you love to do with no interruption. You feel very satisfied if you are able to do this. This time alone bring ideas and creates personal energy. It makes you appreciative of the things you have. It creates a time to know yourself better and to create your personality. This is the time you can work on your personal goals and see your weaknesses. This time also offers you a way to separate yourself from the stresses of your daily routine.

I do most of my thinking and writing when I am alone. I use this time to develop myself, read, and separate myself from the stress of dealing with people and family issues.

Besides time to yourself, it is also important to spend some time with friends who make you happy and make you laugh - someone who you care about, and who cares about you at the same time. It is liberating and satisfying to keep in contact and do some things together. This relationship is the most supportive of any relationship, because your friends, unlike your family members, choose to be around you. These friends are the best people to support you in bad times. However, this relationship is give and take. You receive as much as you give. Finding and keeping good friends makes you feel good.

Cleanliness and Organization:

I personally cannot function well when my surroundings are messy and disorganized. I drop everything and try to start from the beginning. Cleanliness is not only healthy, but it puts you in a good mood. Having some sort of organization at home and at work makes your life easier, as then you won't lose things or have to look for things. Everyone in the family enjoys a clean, organized, and a calm home. For me, just entering a clean room is an instant mood changer and stress reliever.

Solving Problems:

If you are capable of solving a problem, small or big, you should step forward and offer a solution to the problem. At any cost, you should try to avoid adding to the problem or making it harder. It is very rewarding to mediate between two friends or family members over miscommunication or to suggest ways to improve a problem area at work. Ultimately, you will feel the satisfaction of bringing peace, and bringing others to a happy state of mind.

Looking For Beauty All Around You:

Most people forget to include this small piece in their daily routine. Can you really count how many pretty things are in your eyesight? Do you notice the spring's blossoms or fall's colorful trees? Do you notice the blue sky and the white patches of clouds? Do you notice the wet bird under a leaf when it is raining? Do you hear the sound of rain? Do you notice the ants, bees or butterflies or hummingbirds? They are all around you. Try to look for them. Everywhere you are, there is something beautiful to make you feel good and appreciative. If you are inside, try to put images up of things that make you calm and elevate your good mood. I have a photo of the most memorable moment of my Alaska trip in my office. Any time I look at it, it reminds me of the same feeling I had when I was actually there. I felt like that place was the end point of the world, where no one could go beyond those mountains of ice in front of me. Any sadness and stress that I might have instantly disappears.

Take A Trip To A New Place:

To make life interesting, be happy and feel good, it is a very good idea to take a trip to somewhere new. It does not have to be far away or expensive. There are many places in your own area that you haven't seen. Are there new stores in the area? Are there new buildings or a new business? You will have a lot to learn from these new places, and then you can share what you've learnt with your friends and family.

Do Something New:

Yet another way to give yourself a good feeling is to try to do something new that you wouldn't normally do. Cooking a new recipe, knitting a hat or a scarf, painting on canvas, drawing, remodeling the house, painting the walls a different color, or making a piece of jewelry. Any new activity keeps your brain active, creates energy, and puts you in a good mood. I started to learn piano, which is very exciting for me. I take lessons from a wonderful pianist who is perhaps in his eighties. He has spent his whole life in music, and he says I am a good student. I am very confident I will be a good piano player very soon.

Accept Changes:

When I see some people upset, stressed or angry, most of the time their problem is that they don't accept change. New changes happen all the time. You simply cannot be the same person all the time. You have to adapt to change. You grow older, your children grow older, and your needs change from time to time. Accepting change and learning new ways of living means you are ready for anything life brings you. You can act on new things, not react. Optimism, learning, and trying new things always makes you feel good about yourself and keeps your mind and body young.

Refrain From Judging:

Most of the time things are not as they seem. If someone or something doesn't look good to you on the first impression, it is immature to judge and finalize your decision based on that. It is always a good idea to keep an open mind and give room for explanation, or reasons why you didn't like this person or their behavior in the first place. Some people might come across as stubborn and selfish, but when you know them, they are totally the opposite. Not judging someone on the first impression shows your tolerance to variety and diversity. You have to wait until you are sure to make your judgment of either good or indifferent, because experience has shows that things are not as they appear. There is more to every person and every situation.

Being Happy and Laughing:

When I started my piano lessons a couple of months ago, my teacher told me one day that he was looking forward to working with me. He said one thing that he liked about me was that I would laugh when I made a mistake, or when I forgot the notes or his lessons. He promised that I would be a good player very soon. It is very encouraging and feels good to laugh at ourselves, taking life as lightly as possible. I was always told that I have a memorable smile.

Laughing gives you positive energy and puts you in the best mental state. You are happy and put others at ease, which causes them to laugh and be happy. In addition to feelings, I read an article that said some people use laughter to shed stomach fat and give their abs a workout. There are new classes and training sessions especially for seniors called laughing therapy. YouTube videos show people who get together and start laughing. I have yet to try one of these for myself.

Norman Cousins, a political journalist, professor, and author, is a man who laughed his way from sickness to complete health. He had a terminal illness, which the doctors gave him a one-in-five-hundred chance of making a full recovery from. Normal Cousins refused to accept the doctor's opinion and decided to take matters into his own hands. Laughter was one tool Cousins used in a conscious effort to mobilize his will to live and to succeed. He spent most of his time immersed in films, television programs, and books that made him laugh. He eventually recovered completely and wrote his book entitled, "Anatomy of an Illness."

What Withdraws From Your Treasure of Feelings?

Negative feelings like fear, anxiety, stress, pessimism, anger, and jealousy withdraws from your treasure of good feelings. As soon as you have these feelings, you should recognize it and switch gear to change them to positive thinking. When my son takes a little longer to show up at home after work, like any mother, I worry. A Persian phrase says about worry: "Your worst enemy might not say what your conscious says." The best thing I can do at that point is to acknowledge that I am worried and not let all those bad thoughts come to my mind. Instead I imagine my son stopped for a cup of coffee, or some quick shopping, or a haircut. Before I know it, he walks in the door. I knew that I worried for nothing.

Negative feelings make you sad, depressed, vulnerable, dependent, and victim. As a human being you cannot avoid them altogether, but you can minimize time in your sadness, worries, and fear. These feelings are a drain of energy, creativity, and life itself.

They bring pain and disease, and it affects everyone around you.

2nd – Treasure of Feelings – Work Sheet:

Who do you blame for your past misfortunes?

_____

_____

_____

I forgive the following people for my past misfortunes:

_____

_____

_____

I will forgive myself for the following past behaviors:

_____

_____

_____

I will challenge myself and prove I can do the following against other people's opinion of me:

_____

_____

_____

I will strongly and politely say NO to the following requests:

_____

_____

_____

I will take responsibility for the following areas of my life:

_____

_____

_____

I will look for positive points in these situations:

_____

_____

_____

I will volunteer and offer to help the following people or organizations:

_____

_____

_____

I will thank these people today:

_____

_____

_____

I will clean and organize the following areas immediately:

_____

_____

_____

I will share a joke and laugh out loud today with:

_____

_____

_____

I will say YES to doing and trying these new things:

_____

_____

_____

I will stop myself immediately with the following feelings:

_____

_____

_____

2nd – Treasure of Feelings – 7 Daily Reminders:

1. Thank at least one person.

2. Practice deep breathing.

3. Laugh out loud.

4. Think and invite good things into your life.

5. Work on your hobby.

6. Listen to music or play an instrument.

7. Walk to or visit your favorite place.

"Ignorance is the curse of God; knowledge is the wing wherewith we fly to heaven."

William Shakespeare

3rd:

Treasure of Knowledge:

You are born with close to zero intelligence. As you grow older, you add knowledge little by little to know how to deal with your world as you see it. As a child, you learn everything by your senses: watching, hearing, contacting, smelling, and tasting. You actually continue to take all kinds of information using all these senses throughout your life. As you grow older, you draw on past experiences and memories to act accordingly. For the first five years home is your school, and your caretakers and parents are your teachers. After that you need to learn new things, so you go to school and learn how to read, write, calculate, research and think. Twelve years of school teaches you about all different subjects that explains your relationship with this world. This learning experience makes your life easier. As you learn and deposit into your brain, you will then be able to use it anytime in the future.

You graduate high school and continue on to higher education to learn more and get ready for work, a steady income, and settling down. You are ready to have your own family. At this age you seldom use other people's experiences to base your life on. You think you learned how to live and how to deal with everything in your life. You feel you are different from the people of the past and want to find your own path through life.

It might have been enough for ancestors to stay with that first acquired knowledge and live with it for the rest of their lives, but this is not true today. For the past two hundred years, things have changed and people have reached to extraordinary inventions: electricity, cars, planes, satellites, computers, new medicine, and more. Your generation is the information and technology age. Everything changes around you very rapidly and you have to keep up with the changes in order to live based on today's standard of living.

This is the reason for your need to keep learning all of your life. Schools are available and open to everyone.

But aside from school, you need to learn about things that are not taught in schools and that are not part of your major core of study related to your work. You need to keep up with world news, politics, technology, entertainment, sports, and any other things that you are curious about.

How Much Are You Capable Of Learning?

As I said earlier, your brain is capable of holding a lot more information that you use in your lifetime. While it might be a myth that humans use only 10% of their brain, I believe that when humans are put to a test and a great stress, great things happen. This must be the result of a greater concentration and focus in the brain. Learning comes easy and will stay in your memory if you are interested in the subject. This gives you the desire to learn more, do more, and accomplish more. I must conclude that your capability of learning is endless.

Learning Through Education:

There is a class and a mentor for any subject that you would like to study. The starting point is in elementary school and you can go on for as long as you want. You can learn about anything and everything that can be touched, felt, seen, and heard in this world. And then, there is philosophy, astrology, psychology, art, etc. It might be impossible to learn about every subject that there is, but it doesn't hurt if you learn everything that feels important in adding to the quality of life for yourselves and others.

Learning From Reading Current Events:

You learn a great deal from observing others. Current events and news widens your horizon and brings you to the reality of your life. Following the news and trade publications keeps you posted on important issues. It is much easier to have all of this information in the palm of your hands than ever before with today's technology.

Learning From Your Own Research & Questions:

The other way of learning is to find answers to your questions. Your brain is working all day and many questions come across you throughout the day that you would like to find answers to. Again, today's technology makes it possible to find answers. If the Internet does not satisfy you, you can go to specialists and experts on the subject and satisfy your thirst for knowledge.

Learning With Experience:

The hard way of learning is from your own experience. You have to try something to know what it takes. If you have never have been in front of a camera, you wouldn't know how difficult it is. If you have never spoken in public, you never know what it would take. If you have never made a pizza out of scratch, you would not know what to do. The recipe for almost every problem is available in the library, but doing it is instant learning.

It is very timely and inspiring now to know that Thomas Edison had only three months of schooling. He was considered by his teacher, 'too stupid to learn," and was sent home. He was encouraged by his mother to be self-educated and he spent most of his time in the library reading books, especially scientific books. When he was ten years old he set up his own chemical laboratory in the basement of his home. When he was twelve, he took up a job as a newspaper boy. He sold newspapers, candy, books, fruits, and other snacks to passengers of trains. At fifteen, he purchased a small printing press located at the train station. His turning point came when he rescued the son of the railway stationmaster. To show his appreciation to Edison, he taught Edison the art of telegraphy. When he was seventeen, he became one of the most expert telegraph operators. Edison continued to spend time and money on self-improvement and as a result he gained the equivalent of many college degrees, all despite the fact that he had only three months of formal education. Edison realized his weakness and used the engineers, model makers, scientists, mathematicians, and skilled mechanics. During his lifetime he patented more than 1100 inventions. One of his inventions was the electric light bulb. He succeeded only after failing more than 10,000 times.

Learning Through Travel:

Your great learning and wisdom in life comes from being away from your known territory. In fact, many great accomplishments have come as a result of traveling. Experiencing different cultures and different lifestyles broadens your vision and makes you more acceptable of world affairs. Based on great Persian philosophers, traveling is a great way to acquire wisdom.

Learning From Other People:

One of the most important points in your learning process is that you have to use the information that is already available to you by the great men and women of the past. If there is some path that you would like to follow, you should see who has reached greatness in that path and follow that person as a role model. Reading biographies and history books will make it easier for you to mark your own path as you pass through your own life cycle.

Learning From Quotes:

Quotes or words of wisdom have come from thought leaders, great politicians, philosophers, teachers, authors, and speakers. They are the best parts of the best speeches, lectures, and books of the best people. They have survived for thousands of years and will continue to inspire and educate people in the future. I have a collection of quotes and read them regularly. They improve my mood and teach me great lessons on many different subjects. Here are a few time-traveled quotes:

"A life spent making mistakes is not only more honorable but more useful than a life spent doing nothing." George Bernard Shaw, 1856-1950, Playwright

"Parents can only give good advice, but the final forming of a person's character lies in their own hands." Anne Frank, 1929-1945, Writer

"As for worrying about what other people might think - forget it. They aren't concerned about you. They're too busy worrying about what you and other people think of them." Michael le Boeuf, Speaker and Author

"One of the most common causes of failure is the habit of quitting when one is overtaken by temporary defeat." Napoleon Hill, 1883-1970, Author of **Think and Grow Rich**

"Just as a small fire is extinguished by the storm whereas a large fire is enhanced by it - likewise a weak faith is weakened by predicament and catastrophes whereas a strong faith is strengthened by them." Viktor E. Frankl, 1905-1997, Holocaust Survivor and Author of *Man's Search for Meaning*

"Any fool can criticize, condemn, and complain but it takes character and self-control to be understanding and forgiving." Dale Carnegie, 1888-1955, Author and Speaker

"When we set out to do the best we can do, it is inevitable that great opportunity finds us because we are doing what truly makes us happy. We're in alignment and ready for the opportunities that life puts in our path." Josh Hinds, Author of *It's Your Life, LIVE BIG!*

"Above all, be the heroine of your life, not the victim." Nora Ephron, 1941-2012, Journalist, Playwright, Screenwriter and Novelist

"If you want to succeed you should strike out on new paths, rather than travel the worn paths of accepted success." John D. Rockefeller, 1839-1937, Industrialist and Philanthropist

"We will receive not what we idly wish for but what we justly earn. Our rewards will always be in exact proportion to our service." Earl Nightingale, 1921-1989, Author and Syndicated Radio Personality

"Anyone who keeps the ability to see beauty never grows old." Franz Kafka, 1883-1924, Writer

"I began learning long ago that those who are happiest are those who do the most for others." Booker T. Washington, 1856-1915, Educator and Author

"My doctors told me I would never walk again. My mother told me I would. I believed my mother." Wilma Rudolph, 1940-1994, Olympic Gold Medalist

"Steady, patient, persevering thinking will generally surmount every obstacle in search of truth." Nathanael Emmons, 1745-1840, Theologian

"Create a definite plan for carrying out your desire and begin at once, whether you're ready or not, to put this plan into action." Napoleon Hill, 1883-1970, Author of *Think and Grow Rich*

"Be enthusiastic about your decision. It's YOUR decision! Reach, seek, risk! Don't ever stop. Follow your thoughts and don't listen to others. It's your life and you'll get it... You Can Do It!" Sirleny Rodrigues Garcia, Author **of *You Can Do It***

"Not everything that is faced can be changed. But nothing can be changed until it is faced." James Baldwin, 1924-1987, Novelist, Playwright and Poet

"Kindness can become its own motive. We are made kind by being kind." Eric Hoffer, 1902-1983, Author

"The happiness of your life depends upon the quality of your thoughts." Marcus Aurelius, 121-180 AD, Roman Emperor and Philosopher

"The only people you should get even with are those who have helped you." Napoleon Hill, 1883-1970, Author

"You have to believe in yourself, that's the secret. Even when I was in the orphanage, when I was roaming the street trying to find enough to eat, even then I thought of myself as the greatest actor in the world." Charlie Chaplin, 1889-1977, Comic Actor

"If you don't design your own life plan, chances are you'll fall into someone else's plan. And guess what they have planned for you? Not much." Jim Rohn, 1930-2009, Author and Speaker

"Feeling sorry for yourself, and your present condition, is not only a waste of energy but the worst habit you could possibly have." Dale Carnegie, 1888-1955, Author and Speaker

"You may never know what results come from your action. But if you do nothing, there will be no result." Mohandas Karamchand Gandhi, 1869-1948, Led India to Independence

"It's really easy to fall into the trap of believing what we do is more important than what we are. Of course, it's the opposite that's true: what we are ultimately determines what we do!" Fred Rogers, 1928-2003, Creator of Mister Rogers' Neighborhood

"Turning seventy is like beginning the eighth inning of a baseball game. The contest is nearing completion, but there's likely to be some action, and even a few exciting plays, before the game draws to an end." Mardy Grothe, **Author**

"When I thought I couldn't go on, I forced myself to keep going. My success is based on persistence, not luck." Estee Lauder, 1906-2004, Entrepreneur

3rd – Treasure of Knowledge – Work Sheet:

I will learn about the following new subjects:

_____

_____

_____

I will go to the following sources to know more about current world affairs:

_____

_____

_____

I will read these books:

_____

_____

_____

I will read the following people's biographies:

_____

_____

_____

I will enroll in a class to learn the following:

_____

_____

_____

I will document my learned experiences:

_____

_____

_____

I will travel to the following countries to learn more about them:

_____

_____

_____

3rd – Treasure of Knowledge – 7 Daily Reminders:

1. Read the news and current events daily.

2. Read a biography.

3. Learn more about self-development.

4. Find an answer to one of your questions.

5. Read words of wisdom (Quotes).

6. Teach someone what you know.

7. Share ideas and books with your loved ones.

"Just as a candle cannot burn without fire, men cannot live without a spiritual life."

Buddha

4th:

Treasure of Faith:

Faith is a hidden treasure within you. It is your consciousness and your connection to the world. Whether you belong and follow a religion or you are a spiritual person, you rely on an invisible higher power that is beyond your control. This power gives you hope to look at a brighter side of things, to connect with your world, and to call upon when you are desperate. This power is a motivating factor in your life to do well and be good. Faith is an inner power and does not come from the outside. It cannot be forced upon you. It is your beliefs that you have accepted with your mind, body, and heart. You just need to recognize the power of faith with every breath that you take. When you take your faith as your guide to carry on with your life, your body, mind, and emotions become aligned with who you are. You become a person of character, charisma, and knowledge that light up dark rooms as well as dark minds.

Importance of Faith and Connection:

Your lives and your being are all but a puzzle that humans haven't solved yet. There is a much greater system working at perfection to have your universe going. Every little element of this world is there for a purpose and nothing is moving out of place. If you look outside of you, you see the stars, the moon, the planets, the day and night cycle, the rivers, the clouds, the wind, the fires, the earth, the plants, and every breathing being on this earth is here to support life. And, if you look at inside of you, your smallest organs and body cells are working autonomously and unconsciously so you can live. Then there is also the life cycle of every living organism. All animals, plants and humans alike have a birth, growth, and finish cycle, but each group makes sure to produce offspring for continued life in this universe.

Scientifically, there are a lot of unsolved questions in the universe. It is very complicated for the average person to spend time and effort in trying to solve or understand it. Sometimes, it is best to just accept what you have and believe that you simply don't know, and that there is a much higher power, a creator for this world that is looking out for you. It is very comforting to believe your Creator's intentions are that you live in peace and harmony with the universe and with each other. Faith gives you hope and desire to continue on an unknown journey called life because without it, the earth is a dark, cold, scary and empty world with no hope for tomorrow.

If having faith makes you a better human being, what is the harm in believing and following a set of values and principles? This set of values could come from all kinds of faiths that people practice around the world. The final destination is relying in a power that is beyond your understanding and reach. Christians, Muslims, Jews, Hindus, Buddhists, and many other religions of the world have the same messages in different ways. I believe almost half of the world's population realizes this and has an open mind about looking at each of the religions as ways to rely on to the Creator. There is no right or wrong ways to worship, pray, ask for forgiveness, or ask for strength to go on.

Know Your Own Faith:

The faith and the religion that you were born with is the best one to learn, know, and practice. However before practicing it blindly, you must understand everything about your own religion, beliefs, and core values. Most of the time, religions are practiced with cultural and regional traditions that have nothing to do with religion. You have to be able to distinguish what is part of religion and what is part of tradition and society. Almost all of the world's religions have been abused to gain political and financial powers. This abuse overpowers the young and the uneducated who do not know the core of their own religion over the years. Standing up for what is right can be very intimidating and at times very dangerous.

However, I believe that if you are aware of what is right in your religion and what is wrong, no one will be able to victimize you or force you otherwise. You have to believe that your religion should be easy, convenient, and should bring harmony to your life; it's not the other way around. When religion is forced upon and practicing it becomes an involuntary set of chores that is when you are not aligned with true message of your religion. The freedom comes from knowing your own core values that your own religion brings to you.

Knowing and Respecting Other Faiths:

Now that the earth is hitting more than seven billion people and technology has connected us in more ways, the need to understand and respect other faiths is even more necessary. There are valuable lessons and strengths in other religions that help you understand humanity and have a better understanding of your universe. You have to accept diversity and understand that all human beings have the same rights to eat, sleep, pray, and think in their own unique ways. Your way of doing things is not necessarily the right way of doing it. Understanding other faiths deepens your thoughts, imagination, your core values, ethics, and simply leads you to live in harmony with other human beings.

Knowing Yourself:

The importance of faith on your inner world is also very important. It gives you the power to do great things that you never knew was within you. There is a greater reason for your being in this world. There is greater power and greater energy in each one of us than we are using. Most of you are getting very comfortable with an easy superficial routine life without realizing the depth of your being and your full potential. In most cases, spirituality, calmness, and prayer help you know yourself better and to recognize what do you really want to accomplish during your time on this earth.

Living With God Within:

Religion is a way of life. It is a method of living better and making the right decisions. Through religion, you can distinguish right from wrong, as you pave your way into adulthood and parenthood. You become responsible for your own actions. Religion is not a set of rules or rituals that can be only practiced when you have to. I believe if you have the enlightenment of your religion in your heart all the time, you can make better decisions, appreciate life and the things you have, and lead a happier life with regard to your personal and professional lives. If you have the power of God within you all the time, you care for your environment; you see people of less fortunate circumstances than yourself; and you value your time while appreciating your every breath. You will realize that you are not afraid anymore. You will realize that the God within you is empowering. He loves you and nurtures you every step of your life.

Praying and Thinking:

You are living in a time of very fast paced technology. With all the simplicity and convenience that technology should bring you, you find it harder and harder to find a few minutes in your daily time to think, reflect, and connect to your spiritual life. However, in order to have peace and calm in an unsettling time, you need to take some time during the day to reflect, find new strength, count your blessings, and learn from your mistakes. It takes daily practice to acknowledge God within you and feel at peace with your surroundings.

Following Your Core Beliefs And Values – Even If Against the Odd:

Knowing your core beliefs and values enables you to live by your own principles. Respect the rules that are aligned with your own beliefs and stand up for what is right. As human beings, you need to be free to make decisions, make choices, and make your own rules even if it is against odds. This is the power and strength that makes you strong and great human beings. All great leaders of the world have set their own rules to make great interventions in the world.

Telling the Truth:

It is always good to tell the truth so you don't have any extra burden of carrying a load of secrets with you in your memories. Telling lies or hiding the truth is an energy drainer. You always have to spend extra energy to protect the lie that you just said, and you might even have to add more lies to the first one, which will make your load heavier to carry. The best practice is to tell the truth even if it is difficult or even if it is not to your advantage. You will be known as honest and as a person of a good character because you are not living a double-faced life. You are what you are in front of and behind the back of every person you meet.

4th – *Treasure of Faith – Work Sheet:*

I will find answers to the following questions about my faith:

_____

_____

_____

I will practice the following faith related activities:

_____

_____

_____

I will learn about the following other faiths:

_____

_____

_____

I will trust my faith with these situations:

_____

_____

_____

These are the core values that I cannot compromise:

_____

_____

4th – Treasure of Faith – Daily Reminders:

1. Be grateful for your breath.

2. Take time to pray and meditate.

3. Pay attention to your surroundings: clouds, trees, and scenery, and see the power of your Creator.

4. Always trust that things will work out for the best.

5. Listen to your conscious when faced with a tough decision.

6. See the bigger picture and have a bigger vision of in your life.

7. Practice your faith rituals and feel connected.

"Without a family, man, alone in the world, trembles with the cold."

Andre Maurois

5th:

Treasure of Family:

After your own natural and individual treasures, there comes the treasure of your family. Your parents, grandparents, siblings, aunts and uncles, and your extended family are there to support you. Every one of them is a treasure that you can count on for support anytime you need them, and most of the time, they are ready to gives you anything you want. To be able to withdraw from this treasure, you need to nurture your relationship with them as much as possible. Everyone needs to be connected and count on one another to be there and share in their happiness and sadness.

Your immediate family is the strongest asset you have, yet at the same time, you get the most pain from these people. If you cannot understand a person in your family, it is best to accept and love them for who they are and not to expect too much from them. You should not give your family members pain or hurt them in any way. These are people that belong to your family treasure. You cannot change or exchange these people. You cannot change your brother or sister for another one. They are the only family you have and they are unique in their own ways.

Of course you can include everyone who is closest to you into your family treasure circle, whether they are your family, friends, or colleagues. The importance is that the bigger your circle of support, the stronger is your treasure of family. You can look at each one and count on them for help-based on their strengths. But you can only count on them when you are available to serve them, and this is the only way to add to this treasure. The following specific steps will help you add more value to your family treasure.

Accepting Family Members As They Are:

The most pain and discomfort in life comes from the people who are closest to you – your family members. I know many who have complaints about their parents, siblings, coworkers, bosses, and neighbors.

You have to know two facts here: one is that you cannot change anyone to your favor, and two, is that you cannot deny your relationship to a person. Whether you like any one family member or not, they are still family and you will think about them or talk about them for your whole life.

Parents:

Mutual responsibilities need to be shared by the children and the parents in order to have a healthy relationship.

As your role as parents changes when children leave their parents' home, the children's role also changes as they start to build their own lives. They both enter into a new role of close friendship. Their relationship depends on how they enjoy each other's company and how much benefit each one of them receives from their close relationship, or not so close relationship, until there is a time for the children to take care of their parents when they are aging and need support. This is a relationship were they both should find comfort in each other's company. The relationship should be open, mutually beneficial, and without unwanted interference – especially on the part of the parents.

If you are not close to your parents and don't have a mutually beneficial relationship with them, you are not obligated to do anything until it is time that they will need your support when they are old. Then it becomes your obligation. With this being said, parents always have the best intentions for their children and go through many sacrifices for their children while they are growing up. They look to their children to share every minute of their lives with. They count on their children to be an important part of their life to share their happiness and sadness together. They look forward to having grandchildren and enjoying the fruit of their hard work.

If you did not have a good childhood or good memories growing up with your parents, or you grew up without them, then you don't have to necessarily be unkind to them when they need you. This time, it is your choice to do what is right for you and to set an example for your own children. I just believe that parents do their best based on their ability and not all of them have all the answers to go through life. They might have made bad choices while you were growing up and they might have hurt you, but if you ask them now, I bet that they are regretful of what they did.

Siblings:

The real bond among siblings is made as children. They are either their best friends or worst enemies. A good and mutually beneficial relationship between siblings is a blessing that can enrich anybody's life.

This is also another one of those relationships that you cannot change and cannot deny. You have to accept them for who they are, whether you are close or not. It doesn't matter how hard or how easy it was as children, you have a choice to start again as adults. Again, this is a relationship of choice. As you grow up with your siblings in the same house, you all have different personalities with different strengths and weaknesses. You only choose to have connections with the ones who you enjoy the most, to share your life with and raise your children together.

Extended Family:

As long as someone is related to your parents, they are your extended family. You take pride in your family name and look for your family's love, support, and friendship all the time. One fact that plays a role in the role of your extended family is how involved and how much respect this family member earned with your parents. If they were close and you saw them more often while growing up, chances are that you also know them and want to have relationship with. Sometimes it is the mother's extended family and sometimes it is the father's extended family that is closest to the family. However, when you grow up and move on, your relationships start to be open and based on mutual benefits that you give to each other. You keep open, respected, and good relationships with the ones whom you connected with the most. You are not forced to have a relationship if you don't want to, but since they are family you have to accept them for who they are, even if you don't get along.

Friends:

This is a special relationship that happens only because you chose each other to be friends. You relate at some level on your physical and emotional values. This relationship is invaluable in your life. Friends can be your major motivator to do well (and sometimes bad things) in the world. You spend time with them and enjoy that time because you can be yourself with friends. You trust them and confide with them about everything in your life. You rely on their support and advice most of the time. A friend is a person that sometimes is closer to you than your parents, siblings, and family members.

Besides family members, it is crucial to have good friends around you. A friend is someone with whom you can talk and trust, and with whom you always enjoy spending time. Real friends make each other laugh, cry, and give support and advice. Good friends are more than assets in your family treasure. You share your happiness and sadness or even troubles with your friends first. More often than not, you ran away from your family members to your friends for comfort. These are people you chose to be your friends. It is very important to see who your friends are because you are one of them. More often people know you better through your association with your friends. There is a popular and proven word of wisdom to look into here which says if you want to know a person then see whom he or she hangs out with.

It is important to choose friends who can uplift, support and encourages you for the better. Try to stay away from negative people because these relationships are a drain of your energy. Your time, money, and attention are not well spent on people who do not add any value to your life.

Depending on your personality, you can have as many or as few friends as you choose. The most important part is the quality of your relationship. Maintaining relationships often requires your attention, energy, money, and time. Can you give enough time to each one of your friends or you pick a few best friends and have deeper relationship with them? Usually when you are younger, you tend to like to hang out with a lot of people and call them friends, but as you grow older, you will end up with a few that have stuck with you throughout the years. This is normal.

It is also normal for friends to naturally grow apart from each other. Each friendship has its season because things change in your life or your friends' life. It is important to end friendship on a good note because you never know when you may rely on each other again.

One thing that is always important about maintaining your friendships is the balance of your shared responsibilities. If you overpower your friends by demanding that they do things for you, your relationship is not going to last for long. I mentioned earlier that everyone has a serving capacity. Once you push that capacity, the tolerance level will overflow, and everything falls apart. So you have to share responsibilities of carrying on a relationship equally in order for this relationship to be fulfilling. Otherwise, clear communication of your position or feelings will help the other person understand why you are doing what you do.

Community:

You also have a responsibility to your community and those who are serving you. You always have to look out for and have the best in mind for your neighbors. In some cases, especially in emergencies, only your neighbors might be the person available to rush to your aid. Keeping good relations with your neighbors also gives you peace of mind when you are on vacation or away from your home.

Your teachers, banker, grocer, doctor, dentist, hairstylist, mechanic and agents are valuable connections that could grow into a good friendship. You should always treat them well, as they deserve the best for what they do. Believe that they will go an extra mile for you if you do the same for them.

Your politicians, firefighters, police officers, city officials, park rangers, dump drivers, postman are all there to make your life easier and more pleasant. Appreciate their services whenever possible. It only adds to your character to appreciate the people who let you be safe and sleep well at night, and they may spread good words about you.

You should also support your legal system and get involved in choosing your politicians. You should ask questions, get to know them better, and vote for the right person. After all, you need to see if they do their job well by serving people as they promised.

Loving and Helping Others:

The only way you can serve people or have them in your family treasure is to love them and help them in any way you can. By serving, I do not mean that others overtake your life in the pursuit of serving. Everyone has a capacity for serving. If you have deposited into your physical, emotional, intellectual, spiritual treasures, you have much more capacity to be available and to serve without forcing or hurting your own life. However, if someone does not have a good health, that person does not have the capacity to serve. All of the attention and energy should go toward taking care of their health first. However, if a sick person can tutor some kids with math, then that is his or her capacity. So, it is important to know what your capacity is for serving, and to serve as much as possible at any capacity that you can.

Andrew Carnegie was a poor Scottish immigrant boy, barely educated, who started out as a messenger for a telegraph company. Despite humble beginnings he rose to become one of the world's greatest industrialists by the time he was 35 years old, creating America's steel industry and amassing a great fortune, and then later became one of the world's greatest philanthropists. At one time, he had 43 millionaires working for him. Andrew Carnegie believed it was a rich man's duty to give away his money and not die rich. After he retired from steel making, he gave away about $350 million – over $2 billion in today's terms, during the remaining years of his life. Among his many gifts to the United States was a concert hall in New York City, a technical school in Pittsburgh, hundreds of public libraries, and foundations to promote education and research.

Respecting Others As You Want Respect For Yourself:

Sometimes I see people complain of not being respected by another person. Immediately, I become prejudice in my mind and ask the person, "What have you done to deserve this?" Usually the answer is, "I don't know" or "nothing." I believe there is a reason for why people treat you the way they do. This is one thing that I have experimented with, over and over with many people. If you come across as a goofy person, they will be goofy with you. If you make a joke at every opportunity and don't show your serious side, that's what people will remember about you. They will expect you to be the same all the time.

In order to be respected and treated the way you want to be, you have to do the same for the other person. You need to show them who you are and how you like to be treated. People are often very open to this and agree to do whatever it takes if they love you and want you to associate with them. One of my brother-in-laws made it known to everyone that he likes a certain drink and won't drink anything else as a substitute. You know that he likes his food well done and his tea very hot. This is because he has made it known. He gets this treatment for two reasons: one because I like him and want to serve him at every opportunity and two, because he does the same thing for me when he has his chance to serve me. I get ice with my water, I don't smoke his cigar, and I like watermelon and black tea. These are the understood values that we have communicated. However, it is upsetting if I go to his house and he offers me water with no ice and serves me green tea instead of black. Again, I immediately think to myself, "What have I done to deserve this?" The answer is almost always a miscommunication that needs to be taken care of as soon as possible.

Listening instead of Talking:

We are normally very busy with our lives and routine daily chores. Of course, life has its ups and downs in everybody's life. Especially now with the use of technology and social media, grabbing someone's attention is getting harder and harder. Your attention span is shrinking month by month. Most of us tend to talk more than you listen. This is perhaps why some relationships fall apart. If your end goal is to serve people, then you must start with listening. When someone is talking, really listen to what they are saying and respond to their comment versus starting with your own statement. You will definitely strengthen your relationship with that person if you take the time and listen first. There will be plenty of time to talk about yourself after you serve the other person first.

Agreement instead of Argument:

Sometimes you feel like you are the only correct person and what you say is the right thing. You uncontrollably argue with the other person trying to convince them to believe you. In my opinion, argument has never convinced anyone to see it differently. You believe you know as much as you know. If you find value in what you are saying, accept it without argument, and if you feel differently, argument does not make you change your mind. Argument in any case and with anyone is a wasted time that could be enjoyed otherwise.

The moment you find yourself that your conversation is turning into an argument, excuse yourself and make sure to let the other person know that they are entitled to their opinion, whether right or wrong, just as you have the same entitlement. You need to let them know that you will value them but you disagree with their opinion.

Disagreements can be very good – an eye opening conversation – when done constructively. But never turn your conversations into an argument for or against something of which you believe you can convince the other person. On the other hand, chances are that you might not be correct; but at that moment you don't realize it because you are so convinced on being right about the subject. It is always good idea to let the people with whom you disagree know that you value their views and opinions as being different from your own.

When a disagreement turns into an argument make sure to let your point known to the other person and leave it at that, because in the end it might not even be an important subject that you are discussing. You have to understand that you cannot force your opinions onto someone who does not agree with you. It is very normal for others to reject your opinions even though you might be correct. Yet holding an argument with someone on any matter is a waste of time that should be avoided any and all costs.

Praising Instead of Criticizing:

People with positive attitudes always notice the good behavior of others and praise them. Likewise, negative people always complain and try to find something wrong with every situation. Praising brings the best out of everyone and strengthens relationships. You will find joy in praising, whether it is your family member, your kids, your spouse, or someone who you just met. This is an important character trait that is highly rewarding. Try to practice it every day in every situation with everyone you meet. You will then know what I mean.

Listening to Others and Respecting Their Beliefs:

As a proactive person, you have to accept that everyone is entitled to their own opinion and beliefs even if they are not aligned with your opinions. The best thing you can for a relationship is to listen and to accept the other person's beliefs because trying to convince the person otherwise is a waste of time. This wisdom comes in very handy especially if you are dealing with family members. You have to let them know that you love and respect them for who they are, along with their beliefs and opinions. Two good things can come to you as a result: one is that you have to review your own beliefs and see if the other person is right, and two is that now you know a different point of view. If you separate your emotions and accept someone's belief instead of arguing against it, you will end up loving the person and valuing them for their stand of strong opinions. Disagreements with other people broaden your own imagination and opens up more doors into opportunities.

There is a story of the three blind men who came across an elephant. The first one felt the leg of the elephant and said, "An elephant is like a tree trunk." The second blind man felt the ear of the elephant and said, "No, no, the elephant is like a big fan." The third blind man touched the trunk of the elephant and said, "Both of you are wrong! An elephant is in fact like a big snake!" All of the three blind men were correct in their explanation of the elephant based on their own information. Just remember that in life we may interpret situations differently from others, and just because we see things differently does not mean that others are wrong. We see things according to our beliefs, values, and references, which we pick up along the way in our journey through life.

Being Happy and Laughing:

If you want others to like you, relate to you, and trust you, you must be a happy person. Genuine happiness comes to a person from good health, good feelings, and good faith. This is a trait that makes people comfortable and feels good. Of course, life has its ups and downs, and you will find times that you are not just happy, but if you tend to carry on with your sadness and imperfect life with others most of the time, it eventually overwhelms others. Keep in mind that all bad situations are temporary and it will move on.

Living Alone:

We are always dependent on each other to live collectively. It doesn't matter which country we are in or who we are living with, as long as we associate with other people, then our needs have to be met. We need to share our happiness, sadness, problems, ideas, wealth, and wisdom to be happy and satisfied. People who are living alone do not have a chance to share much if they are not socially active. They actually become more dependent on their own. They become lonely and it shows on their bodies and minds. Depression is a major disease that can occur as a result of loneliness. Overall, it is just not safe to live alone. People who live alone are living a shorter life.

However, some people are forced to live alone, especially at the start of young adulthood and at the end of your life at old age. If you are living alone and you are happy then make sure you are staying connected with your neighbors, friends, family, and children. Someone has to know your whereabouts in order for you to be safe and protected, especially in old age.

Choosing Your Partner/Spouse:

This is the most important relationship that belongs to your social treasure. It is the one ultimate relationship that makes your life a heaven or a hell. I'm talking about the person you will share yourself with on many levels – your spouse. You need to rely and depend on a trusted person to take care of you and be on your side. This makes you happy and is the only way to fully enjoy life. This person is very important in your life. You will build your family with this person, so you better have the right person to start with. You need to have similar interests and values, and be compatible physically, emotionally and intellectually.

Of course this is everyone's dream, but often times it does not happen right from the start. This relationship can grow and become mutually a loving and caring relationship if the couple chooses to make it happen that way.

The married life is always a roller coaster of ups and downs as the couple is raising children. However, you also have to realize that with time, people's needs, desires, and goals change. Many couples stay with each other based on core values and shared interest through tough times. In any situation, they have respect for each other, love each other unconditionally, and try to make a happy life for and with each other.

A compatible spouse adds to quality of life and all of your treasures: physical, emotional, intellectual, spiritual, social, occupational, and financial. Having someone close to your heart that you enjoy spending time with adds years to your life, not to mention that happy couples raise well-rounded and healthy children together.

There always have to be a balance of power between husband and wife. Otherwise one of them gets overpowered which breaks the balance and everything will eventually fall apart.

Sometimes you have to work a little harder to fall in love with your spouse by changing your perception and looking at all the good points, all the happy moments of life. You should be understanding, fair, and open to communications. You should be fun, creative, and supportive to be with, and create a nurturing atmosphere for everyone in your family to be safe and comfortable.

If you find that your mind is always at fight with your spouse and you have differences in your core values that are unsolvable, then there is no reason to go on living a miserable life together. You will never know what a happy life is like if you stay in an unhealthy relationship. You deserve to be happy and find someone who can make you happy to share life with them.

When you are in an argument or disagreement with your spouse, never use harsh and demeaning words whether you stay with your spouse or separate. You have a choice not to get mad and angry to the point of losing your temper and control. So choose your words carefully because they can haunt you later, and it hurts the other person not only at that moment but for a long time afterwards.

However, before deciding to do a separation, think really hard if you are making the right decision. These are some tips that will help you with your decision. Ask yourself if you really love this person despite all the negative points that he or she might have. One fact is that no one in this world is a perfect person, without flaws, that can sweep you off your feet all the time. You have to deal with all the negative points of your spouse only if you have a strong-shared core value that you love about this person. This is because you might not be able to find another person like the one you've already got. Clear communication between both of you could also help resolve your differences.

What Kills Relationships?

Backstabbing and gossip: Never catch yourself talking negative about anyone because it is just a waste of your time. Gossip does not add anything to your life or the life of the other person, and never let anyone talk negative about someone else either. This personality adds to your character as an honest and strong person who can say good and bad things in front of the person and not behind their back. Also know that someone who gossips about someone to you, will gossip about you to someone else. Always be careful not to say something that could embarrass you later.

Jealousy: jealousy is different from competition. Never feel jealous about someone's success and happiness. Be happy wholeheartedly for someone who has achieved something great and is happy about it. Jealousy shows on your face and your body when you feel it. This is a feeling that will not let you enjoy your present moment.

Yes, other people's success and achievement can become the cause of your motivation to become competitive and do your best in whatever you do, to achieve higher and better results. But this has to come from your own hard work, dedication, and talent, not because of gossip, backstabbing, or jealousy. You will enjoy your own success and enjoy sharing it with someone who really is happy for you.

Complainers: You are wasting your time on negative remarks, comments, and statements of which you cannot have any control for improvement. You cannot convince complainers to take action and solve their own problems because it is sometimes just their habits. If it is a person that you care about, you need to let them know that you will not be able to continue your relationship with them because of negative conversations, and give the person some time to improve this bad habit. Or, if this is your friend and he or she tries to take some load off onto you on a temporary basis, it is okay to be patient and listen. However, if this becomes a recurrent habit, it is best to avoid this person altogether.

Selfishness: A lot of people achieve financial success by being very selfish. It means that they have to manipulate others, and take advantage of others for their own personal gain. This is selfishness, which can only work for a short time. If financial success is your only goal, you will succeed; but if you want to live a purposeful life, you will be fair and balanced in treating other people – even people who know less than you or have less than you.

Over Expectation: Do you expect others to be there for you and do things for you when you don't do the same for them? You expect others to solve your problems and go the extra mile for you – sometimes demanding and sometimes begging. You have to realize that everyone is busy with their own life and might not be available all the time to be with you and respond to your needs.

Often times you are making a lot of assumptions and make your expectations based on that. You have to realize that other people – even family members – are not obligated to fulfill your expectations. You should accept that it is their choice only to do if they do, and just be appreciative.

Many families, especially parents, suffer when their kids don't do as they expect them to do. Again, the best thing to do is not to expect favors from others, and you should not make any assumptions of why they are not capable of not meeting your expectations. This is the best way to have long lasting relationships.

You save yourselves from a lot of disappointment if you don't expect people to do favors for you. And if they do as you expect, consider it a bonus for your good behavior, personality, and your relationship; it does not work that way all the time. When things do not go your way, don't dismiss people right away. Always give them a second chance to explain their position. You can either accept or reject their explanation. But fighting with the person never solves the problem.

Being Unfair: Occasionally, our relationship breaks because we treat others unfairly. We use their time, money, and talent without letting them know, or without compensation. It is one thing to be known as smart or as a go-getter, but you never want to be known as unfair and selfish.

We also don't want to let other people take advantage of us for no reason. We always say "Yes" because we are a good person and want to be liked and trusted, but we have to have our own best interest in mind and sometimes politely say "No" if we are asked to do something unexpectedly that we are not capable of doing. We take away time, energy, and money from our own goals and dreams in order to serve other people's unfavorable requests.

5th –Treasure of Family Work Sheet

Who are the most important people in your life?

_____

_____

_____

Who do you count on in times of trouble?

_____

_____

_____

Who do you share your happiness with right away?

_____

_____

_____

Who should hear you say, you love them?

_____

_____

_____

Who do you need to apologize to or have unfinished business with?

_____

_____

_____

Who do you see as a good leader or role model?

_____

_____

_____

Who counts on you and calls on you all the time?

_____

_____

_____

I value the following traits in my spouse:

_____

_____

_____

I will have to spend more time with the following friends:

_____

_____

_____

I will have to improve myself in the following areas:

_____

_____

_____

5th – Treasure of Family – 7 Daily Reminders:

1. Be in touch with all the important people in your life.

2. Arrange for time to be spent with someone you love.

3. Solve a problem or a miscommunication.

4. Volunteer and give your genuine advice to help someone.

5. Tell someone you love them.

6. Thank or praise someone.

7. Ask for help.

"But the problem is that when I go around and speak on campuses, I still don't get young men standing up and saying, 'How can I combine career and family?'"

Gertrude Stein

6th:

Treasure of Career:

Your career can be your best asset or your worst liability. The purpose here is to build your career as an asset for yourself. We all need to work and bring in income for survival. You cannot depend on others to provide this for you. Most people work more than half of their lives. You start working from your teenage years, and some people will keep working past retirement age. On one hand, your life expectancy is longer and on the other hand, job and careers have changed from having one long and steady job to having more challenging and short-term jobs.

Choosing a career that you like is an asset because the more you invest in it, the more your skills and talents for productivity and performance will increase. The most difficult job is finding and preparing for the work that you are passionate about.

How Do You Choose Careers?

When you are looking for a job, you usually get what you can instead of hoping and waiting for your desired position or career. If you have a choice to choose, these are the three things that people choose to work for:

1. Money

2. Passion

3. Cause

4. Survival

Choosing a career based on generating income is not an ideal way of work. A job has to reward you both financially and emotionally. You might be able to make a lot of money, but in the end, you don't enjoy your job. Chances are that you work long hours and sacrifice a lot physically and socially to gain momentum in your job. What will happen if you lose your job, or if your income is not there to support your lifestyle? A good friend of mine, whose sole intention is to make lots of money, suffered two strokes in the last five years. You have to be careful because money can have negative affects your health, feelings, and family.

Jobs for money: business, banking, investing, manufacturing, and sales.

You will only be happy if you choose your career for based on your passion, and for a cause that you are passionate about. However, sometimes it is hard to generate income when choosing to do something with passion. It is definitely hard to start a career that requires some investment in education or capital investment. However in the long run, this is the best thing that you can do for your life.

Jobs for passion: consultant, artist, entrepreneur, self-employment, and teacher.

When you work for a cause, you have a mission. You are not looking for money, power, or fame. You want to help and serve. Politicians, firefighters, policemen, religious leaders, and non-profit organizers are all working for a cause. Their job is to serve people in a selfless manner, yet sometimes they get into trouble for greed and power. So make sure that if you choose a career for a cause it is for the right reasons.

Jobs for a cause: Politician, media, military, firefighter, police officer, and priest.

If you are working for survival, it really doesn't matter what you do. You need to generate income and provide for yourself and your family. Almost everyone has held a job that was for this purpose. These jobs should be only held for a short time until you find your real career and do something that is according to your talent and passion. Many feel that there is no other way out of their unsatisfying jobs. You have to believe in yourself that you were born to do more and live a better life. This section of the book will help you get out and reach your goals.

Jobs for survival: employment, odd jobs, and blue-collar jobs.

There are many good and well-respected jobs for everyone to make a living. However, some people make poor choices with their careers. They might not know the consequences now, but will regret it for the rest of their lives. Stay away from careers like drug dealing, illegal trafficking, prostitution, theft and gambling that will not make you or your family proud. Don't do anything illegal that will get you in trouble with the law. Always ask yourself what are better choices for you to make money. You have to realize that your job and career affects your family as well.

What You Were Made to Do?

When you were still in middle school or high school, you had a pretty good idea of what you were going to be when you grow up. Some followed through with it by going through the right path of study in college and then worked at a dream job or career. Most of the time, we grow apart from our dream job/career for various reasons. Usually this dream stays with us for the rest of our lives until it is fulfilled.

If you choose something from an early age, you have an advantage of succeeding tremendously in your career. You have more time and opportunity for improvement and adaptability. If you don't have an idea of what to do and have not found your passion for work early in life, you are at a disadvantage and at risk for wasting some time. If you are confused about your career choice, it is best to start looking and thinking hard, to start from where you are today and plan for your dream career in the near future. You can start any time with a new career!

My first dream job was to be an English teacher back in my high school years. I was living in Afghanistan where most of the population is illiterate and the main language is Farsi. I wanted to open a new door of opportunity for people to communicate in the most dominant language of the world. Unfortunately, my life course has changed with the war and I drifted apart from this dream as well as from many other ones. For many years now, I have been trying unconsciously to go toward teaching. Now, it is more clear to me than ever. I attended college to get my Bachelor of Arts degree and work toward my masters so that I will earn my teaching credential.

You will need to dig deep to remember or find out, what your favorite job in the world is, and make concrete plans to make it a reality in your life. Think of a person that you believe has a job or career that would be a dream-job for you. Research the industry and the job and see if it really is as good as it looks. Sometimes, the most glamorous jobs are the most stressful and most difficult jobs to do. However, you have to realize that the most challenging jobs should have the most rewards for your personal and financial satisfaction.

If you are still confused, you can go online to the Small Business Administration's site and look through a very long list of careers. You will find more than thirty thousand different jobs to choose from. Make a list of your favorite ones and then pick the top three choices. Research the industry, position, investment, and benefits of that job. Then find a person who is at the top of their industry, or currently working that job and do some more research. Read their biography and find out how they got to where they are now.

Once you find what you should do for life as a career, then there are other issues that you need to keep in mind as well.

The other option is to improve on what you are doing now. You already have experience working on the job, and you do it better than anyone else. Think of ways to improve it, and make it your dream job and career.

What Does Your Job Tells About You?

We all find fame, fortune and satisfaction from our job and what we do. We have to be proud of what we do and do it with passion. There are obvious and not so obvious stereotypes with our job and career. We need to make sure that it is the best representation of our personality that brings the best of us out to serve others.

These are some examples of what your job will tell about you:

Teacher: school/classroom environment, intellectual, calm, leader, proud, low income, reader, author, missionary, philosopher, and thinker.

Doctor: work in hospital with sick people, busy, liable, germs, smells, uniform, long hours of work, overtime and weekend work.

Mechanic: workshop environment, grease, oil, car parts, work with tools, deals with drivers with car problems, uniforms.

Office Worker: works in cubical, set hours, routine schedule, works with telephone and computers, office politics, deals with co-workers, papers, policies, attend meetings.

This is meant to be an internal exercise for you to know your job better. It is in no way to think about what others see about you. It is the least bit of importance what others think about what you do, except for your spouse and your children. Your family is supposed to live with your career choice, and it does not affect anybody else in the world. Your job will bring you satisfaction, pride, and money if you like what you do. It will show your strengths and bring out the best of you. You will enjoy your life and do your job with enthusiasm and passion.

When my son told me that he wanted to become a chef, I had series of questions for him. He has never worked in a kitchen before. So, I told him that I don't have any problem if he goes to a culinary school and gets a private education that will cost him more than more than sixty thousand dollars, if he could manage to work in a commercial kitchen for six months before that. My goal was for him to understand that being a chef is not only about creating nice plates of food, but also working in a dark and hot kitchen in front of a burner or oven. If after all that becoming a chef was what he wanted, he could then choose this career consciously and will become a pretty good chef.

Doing the work that you love will bring variety to your life and will save you from boredom. Imagine yourself working in a cubical working the same hours, same activities, with same people every day for a few years. It does not sound very interesting. However if you are working with passion and creating something with your hands, working with different objects and different people every day, how exciting your life could then be.

How Your Job Affects Your Family:

It is very important to do what you love to do. This way it feels as if you are never working. You do your best job with passion and serve others the best possible way that you could serve. As a result, you are rewarded for your specialties and skills. Your job should bring you two kinds of rewards at the same time: emotional and financial. In order for you to be successful, you need to have the support of your family behind you. Some jobs require traveling and time away from your family; is this okay with you and your family? Some jobs require you to work long hours, weekends and holidays; it this okay with your family? If your spouse and children suffer from something that you do because of your job, you need to make a decision to change your job or somehow make a compromise. You have to remember that your job is the way that you can provide for your family for their ultimate happiness. If they are not happy with what you do, you could be doing the wrong thing, or you haven't communicated clearly with them.

If you are married, you need to consult with your spouse to make sure you have their agreement and support for what you do. Otherwise, frustration builds up and it can cost your peace of mind, and eventually cost you your family. My friend is married to an ER physician. He is on-call most of the time and may need to be at work at any time. My friend either isolates herself from parties or is by herself most of the time. She does not spend much time with her husband and they don't have time to enjoy the money that he is making. Although she is proud of his occupation, she deals with loneliness that is associated with his career. As it looks now, they will eventually be faced with bigger problems if they decide to have kids and build a family together.

Learning Ways to Enhance Your Career:

It doesn't matter what you do, but if it is something you do all the time, you need to improve it by reading books, brainstorming, attending classes, and researching the Internet. You need to have the latest information and technology for your career to maintain your success and position.

Allen, a woodcutter, was employed in a timber company for ten years, yet he never got a raise. The company later hired Richard to do the same job. However, Richard got a raise within the first twelve months. Allan was disappointed and decided to approach the management of the company. He was told that his production had never increased over the last ten years. On the other hand, Richard had cut more trees in the period of just one year. The company promised to give Allan a raise if his production went up. He went back to work and tried harder but unfortunately his results did not improve. One day he happened to meet Richard and decided to ask for Richard's advice. Richard told Allan that after he cut down a tree, he would take a short break to sharpen his axe. Allan suddenly realized that he was too busy cutting down trees that he failed to take a break to sharpen his axe.

It is important to take a break from the pressure of work to go on a holiday once in a while. Spend some time on self-development to renew our body and mind, to become more productive.

You should have a system of learning something new all the time. Meeting people, studying competition, and adapting to change are mandatory for being successful in what you do. Otherwise, you will fall behind.

Changing Careers:

The days of working a long time for one company are gone. People are changing careers very frequently – sometimes every three to four years. The need for each person to know more and do more is greater than ever before.

Colleges offer courses and degree programs that just were not around in the last four years. New classes are introduced based on new demands. New graduates can be a twenty-year-old or a eighty-year-old person. For this reason, it is never too late to change career or improve what you do. There are no obstacles except the ones we make for ourselves.

Attar, a third-century Persian poet and philosopher, once said, "Escaping from any prison is possible, but the imaginary prison that you have made for yourself is what you live in." When you leave this imaginary prison, you will find your wings to fly above the valleys and look down upon everything else. In other words, everything that you believe about yourself, your job and your life could be based on your own imagination. If you are not satisfied with who you are and what you do, don't be afraid to change it and make a new life for yourself. All you need to do is to find out what you want, make a goal and follow through on it.

Setting and Keeping Goals:

In order to go where you want to go, you need a plan and a vision. Your plans could change because your needs change, but having no plan is a plan for failure and being lost.

Your plans need to be ambitious enough to challenge you. If your goals are too small, you will get bored with them, and if they are too big, you get frustrated and quit in middle of the way to achieving them. The best thing is to make an attainable goal for the short term, medium term, and long term. Your short-term goal should be for three to six months, the medium-term goal should be for one to three years, and the long term would then be for three to five years.

Your goals need to be clear and concise with specific details to work out. They have to have a date by which you need to accomplish them. They also needs to have actionable small steps that you can take every day to get one step closer to your dreams and goals. For instance, if my goal would be to travel to New York, it might not happen until I have clear actionable steps and a date by which I need to take action. My goal should look like this, which makes it promising:

3. Travel to New York at the end of October.

4. Save $200 every month for the next three months in order to purchase the airfare.

5. Book a hotel in September, 30 days before my departure to get the maximum savings.

There was an experiment conducted on the Processionary Caterpillars. These caterpillars would blindly follow the one in front of them. The caterpillars were carefully arranged in a circle around the rim of a flowerpot, so that the lead caterpillar came into contact with the last one, thus making a complete circle. Some pine needles, the food of the processionary caterpillars, were placed in the middle of the flowerpot. The caterpillars went round and round for seven days and seven nights, and finally dropped dead of starvation and exhaustion, ironically, with abundance of food within reach. Like the processionary caterpillars most of us are going round and round like a merry-go-round, achieving no concrete results, although there are abundance of opportunities everywhere. We confuse activity with accomplishment just like the caterpillars. We may be busy doing many things, but without fruitful results because we are more "wandering generalities" rather than being "meaningfully specific." We must have specific goals and objectives if we are to live meaningful lives.

At the end of this chapter, I am including a list of all career and occupations listed on the United States Bureau of Labor and Statistics Department website (http://www.bls.gov/k12/azlist.htm). You can get detailed information about each one of the following opportunities:

Accountant
Actor
Actuary
Agricultural and food scientist
Anthropologist
Architect
Artist
Automotive mechanic
Bookkeeping clerk
Budget analyst
Carpenter
Chemist
Childcare worker
Civil engineer
Coach
Computer hardware engineer
Computer support specialist
Cost estimator
Court reporter
Dancer
Database administrator
Designer
Desktop publisher
Drafter
Economist
Editor
Educator
Electrical engineer

Electrician
Environmental scientist
Farmer
Financial analyst
Firefighter
Fitness trainer
Historian
Human resources assistant
Judge
Landscape architect
Lawyer
Librarian
Loan officer
Mathematician
Microbiologist
Musician
Paralegal
Pharmacist
Photographer
Physician
Physicist
Police officer
Professional athlete
Psychologist
Real estate agent
Recreational therapist
Referee
Registered nurse
Reporter
Secretary
Social worker

Software developer
Statistician
Surveyor
Systems analyst
Urban planner
Veterinarian
Web developer
Writer
Zoologist

6th – Treasure of Career – Work Sheet:

I wanted to have the following job(s) when I was a child:

_____

_____

_____

I would like to bring about these changes to enhance my current job or career:

_____

_____

_____

I would like to know more about the following careers:

_____

_____

_____

What would I do if money were not an object?

_____

_____

_____

Can you create a business from the above list?

_____

_____

6th –*Treasure of Career – 7 Daily Reminders:*

1. Show up to work.

2. Do more than you are expected within your job or career.

3. Solve problems and help others.

4. Work with passion and love your job.

5. Take steps to improve at least one thing about your job.

6. Learn about other careers.

7. Read your industry journal or trade magazine.

"The greatest wealth is to live content with little."

Plato

7th:

Treasure of Wealth:

Financial wealth is my last treasure and the least important of all the seven treasures. For some people, this comes in first place because they work so hard without regards to their health, emotions, or family. This is my core belief: when you are in good health, feel great, see possibilities, have the intellect to make the right decisions, are spiritually connected to know right from wrong, have a supporting family and a job that you love, that money will come its way into your home. If you have enough deposits into the six treasures above, you might have all the financial wealth you think you need. This being said, I still believe that money is important for buying your necessities. You don't want to depend on others for your expenses. For this reason, I am including my common knowledge about wealth, hoping to guide you in the right direction.

My goal is that you find the value of money in your life; talk about it with your spouse and kids. Hopefully you will teach your children from an early age to play with money and know everything about money that there is to know. We usually shy away from talking about money. This is not healthy for a responsible family. Many relationships break because of money. I hope that you take this matter seriously to communicate how you feel about money with your spouse and family, and make money decisions together.

Know the Value of Your Money:

For an example from the greatest American industrialist and philanthropist, John D. Rockefeller, his children received 25 cents per week plus they had the opportunity to earn additional money by growing vegetables or raising animals. He also required each of his five sons to record their expenses. According to Nelson, one of the Rockefeller children, the boys had control over their money but were asked to give 10 percent of their earnings to charity and to place another 10 percent into savings. They had to balance their accounts every month by accounting for each penny, listing where and how they spent it. Later on, Nelson Rockefeller became the governor of New York and later rose to the position of Vice President of the

United States. One of his brothers, David, became the chairman of Chase Manhattan Bank. David had said that all of the brothers benefited greatly from this exercise in controlling their own money.

Your relationship with money is learned by watching how your parents dealt with their money. Was money very important when you were growing up? Were there fights over money? Have you become closer or grown apart around money while growing up? I am asking these questions because you don't learn anything about money anywhere except for from the home. There's not one subject in our entire time in school to teach us how to budget and how to value our hard earned money. Our capitalist society is always about spending. You are really pushed to spend more than you make. You are even given free money that you don't yet have, with credit cards so you can "freely" spend. Credit card companies are trying to own a chunk of your unearned income in advance. And the majority of the population is not educated enough to make the right decision about their finances.

Many work really hard to earn an income and provide for their families. They make good money, but the hardest part is keeping the money. I can relate this to two types of behaviors: one is that we don't know the value of the money, and two is that we spend it without any budget and make impulse purchases. For this reason, you end up without money before your next paycheck.

There are some people who love their money so much that all they do is save. They don't spend their money out of fear of the unknown, and have no clear plan of what to do with their money. Yes, money has a value, but not so much that you deprive yourself of the beautiful things that you can enjoy only at your age. I have to say for these people, that the real commodity most value is your age and your time. If you don't enjoy your time and age presently, what are you saving the money for without a solid goal? If you are saving for buying a house, great; if you are saving for buying a car, great; if you are saving for a vacation, great. But spend it when the time comes, and then go on to the next milestone in your life.

So think about what is the value of money to you. Think hard about your childhood and how you thought money would play a role in your life. Did you always dream to have a lot of money? Did you think that money could buy you happiness? Do you see yourself a failure when you are in the presence of a rich person? Be honest with yourself because if you love money and that making a lot of money is your goal, then it is possible to go after it and make it happen. You might not be able to deposit into your other treasures as much as your financial treasure, but that is your choice. Go for it for a short time and make it your goal. There is nothing wrong with that. And if for any reason it does not happen for you in the first couple of tries, don't kill yourself on the way to being wealthy.

Robert Allen, in *Multiple Streams of Income*, introduced me to these seven money skills. The first three of them are the foundation for all financial success. Without them none of the other skills have power. They are:

1. Value it – don't waste it on things you don't need.

2. Control it – have a budget and know where and how you will spend it.

3. Save it – reward yourself from your income first.

4. Invest it – let your money make money for you.

5. Make it – always look for more ways to generate income.

6. Shield it – protect your money from lawsuits and more taxes.

7. Share it – always share a little of your wealth.

Pay Yourself First:

For some people, the way to financial wealth starts with saving small amounts of money out of their paychecks. It really does not matter how big or small your paycheck is; if you always spend less than what you make, you will be able to put some money aside.

You can save this money for emergencies, investments, planned projects, or just a peace of mind in case you lose your job or something happens to you. There are two major benefits with paying yourself first: one is that you will save for your future, and the other is that you don't spend more than you make. If you spend more than you make, you will never be able to catch up and reward yourself with what you deserve.

Pay All Your Debts:

When you don't have debt, it means that you have control of your actual money. You decide what to do with your money – not your credit card company. Try to stay away from debt if at all possible. Go through a plastic surgery. By that I mean, take a scissors and cut all of your credit cards in pieces, and throw them out in the garbage. The only debt you want to have is for your home and perhaps for your car. However if you use credit cards to purchase something, make sure you have the money set aside at the end of the month to pay in full for that purchase. You need to understand that minimum monthly payments on your credit cards will keep in you in debt forever. You will end up paying twice or triple for your purchase. Try to pay as much as you can to pay off all of your debt so you can start your own financial freedom, and this is the way to do it.

If you have a lot of debt that you feel you would not be able to pay off any time soon, or your income does not support paying large amounts toward the debt every month, you could consider filing for bankruptcy. Bankruptcy is the secret tool of the wealthy against huge debt that people cannot pay. This service is also available for you to wipe out all of your debt so you can start over. All you need to do is contact a bankruptcy attorney and schedule a consultation to see if you qualify.

Follow A Budget:

With budget, you never run out of money. You need to have a plan for your own money as soon as you have it. After paying yourself first, pay all your fixed expenses like your rent or mortgage, car payment, gas, and electricity bills. Then set aside money for your food and gas expenses for the remainder of the time before your next paycheck comes. If you find that you have more than what you could spend on necessities, you will know the exact amount and you will know what to do with it. Some people add it to their savings, some save it for a bigger projects like a long vacation, and some spend it on Starbucks, Jamba Juice, or that electric ice cream maker that you don't need. The choice is yours.

Here is a list to help you with budgeting:

- Shop with a list only.

- Change your bank if you find a bank with lower fees.

- Don't use ATMs if there are extra charges.

- Pay the balance of your credit cards in full.

- Shop for lower premium insurance.

- Choose to have high deductible with your insurance.

- Buy generic medications instead of brand names.

- Check your receipts for mistakes and overcharges.

- Rent the things you use only once or twice instead of buying and storing them.

- Shop for a lower long distance telephone company.

- Don't pay extra for some features like call forwarding or caller id if you don't use them.

- Use emails instead of telephone calls.

- Rent a movie instead of going to the movie theater.

- Cook your meals at home instead of going out.

- Take your lunch with you from home instead of buying one.

- Borrow your books and magazines from the library instead of buying them.

- Go to a park for relaxation – it's free.

- Use a carpool instead of driving your own car to work every day.

- Buy your air travel tickets far in advance to save.

- Use coupons and reward cards for shopping.

- Buy things that you always need to use in bulk.

- Wash your own car.

- Wear a sweater instead of raising the heat level in your house.

- Make your doors and windows energy efficient.

- Wash full loads in your dishwasher or clothes washer.

- Use your own insurance when renting instead of buying new insurance.

- Use shopping bags for your garbage cans instead of buying garbage bags.

- Use cloth towels in your kitchen instead of paper towels.

- Have a piggybank for the change around your house.

- Save $1 for yourself every day.

- Invest your raise from your job instead of spending it.

- Turn off lights and appliances when not in use.

Protect Your Assets:

As much as valuing our hard earned income, you also need to protect the value of the expensive things you have bought with your money. For instance, you buy expensive clothing, then you put them in the washing machine to get ruined; you buy an expensive piece of rug for your living room, and you walk on it with dirty shoes; you buy an expensive piece of furniture, then you spill food on it; you buy an expensive car, and you don't maintain it regularly. I hope you got my message. Everything that is around you is your assets and if you protect them well, they will last a long time. Then you won't have to spend more money to buy another asset or repair the ones you have.

If you pass over the small stuff for a moment, know that your biggest assets are your home and your car. Protect them by buying insurance for them. If something happens to the house or car, insurance can take care of a large amount of damage. Speaking of insurance, you also should insure your health and life for that matter. The cost of getting medical treatment is too high, and can put anyone at risk of losing all of your assets.

Keep A Good Credit Score:

The United States and many industrialized countries offer credit to people based on their spending habits. If you spend your money wisely and have the integrity to pay back your debt, the banks offer you more credit. If you could use $1500 credit in the beginning of any project and you proved your credit worthiness, you can have access to unlocking more and more credit. This means that the credit card companies trust you will pay them back all of their money plus interest.

You always should try to keep your good credit score to be able to have access to bigger amounts of money that you don't currently have. Your credit score is used to get better deals when you buy a house, a car, or even to get better employment. It also can be a good source of emergency cash that you could have when you need it.

It is a good practice to check your credit score occasionally and find out your credit history. This is done to make sure there are no inaccuracies. Experian, TransUnion, and Equifax are the three major credit bureaus that will have all your financial and employment background. It costs a small fee for you to access your reports and credit score online.

Saving For Emergencies:

You always have to be prepared for emergencies that disrupt your daily routine. In an emergency, whether personal or natural, you need to rely on this account to get you through until you can go back to work. If you have this account, you don't have to rely on anyone else for your basic needs. So you need to set aside a separate savings account and deposit a portion of your income in this account for those rainy days.

Saving For Retirement:

It is your own responsibility to think about your old age when you cannot work. The cost of living will be higher than now, and you need a steady income to pay for your necessities. The government retirement plan, the social security contributions, will not pay enough to support your lifestyle. Even if you have to live below your means, you will not be able to live independently. Retirement planning is like a savings plan that you pay now and reap the rewards later. It is an asset account that you don't pay taxes on when you are younger.

Your money will grow and earn interest year after year. Although most retirement plans have one purpose, there are different ways and different accounts. You need to research to know which one fits your lifestyle and how much you want to set aside.

Saving For Investments:

As you went through above, it is very important to start investing from your savings account as early as possible. Your investment in real estate or the stock market requires a learning curve. If you can do it yourself, it is a good idea to be sure of what you are doing so you don't take on risks for losing your seed money. Always have a strategy and invest with the purpose of making extra money. You only can do this if you have extra money set aside. So maybe you can skip your one long vacation and plunge into an investment. The sooner you start is the better. There are plenty of books and resources to learn more about the right investment for you. The first step is to put some money aside for this purpose only.

Generating Income:

Based on the famous book of Rich Dad's, *A Guide to Investing*, by Robert Kiyosaki, there are four sources from which you can make money:

1.   Employment

2. Self-Employment

3. Business Investment

4. Investment

The least amount of money is made from employment. You have to let someone else use your talent and your time in exchange for a paycheck. The government also takes out a portion of your paycheck, and you will pay most taxes through income tax as well. A majority of the population is employed.

With self-employment you are working for yourself. You make as much as you work and make as much as you charge per hour or per project. You report your income with your income tax filing and pay a self-employment tax to the government.

When you invest in a business, you invest in a system to make money for you. You hire employees; invest in equipment, space, and tools to offer a service or product. There is no limit on how much you make because it depends on your market size and product. Most of the companies are formed as a business, which is a separate entity than the person who owns it. There are two different ways of establishing businesses: Corporations and Limited Liability Companies. Both of these business structures pay their own taxes to the government and the owners are not personally liable for losses of the business.

The last source of income and the most rewarding is investment. This is where your money is working for you and bringing you income. This is through stocks, bond, commodity, currency, precious metals or real estate investments. When you save money, then you have the opportunity to invest your money to generate more income.

Now you know who makes money and how it is generated. Employment and self-employment is an active form of generating income while business and investment is passive method of generating income. You work in exchange for money in active form, and your investment generates income for you in the passive form. We all want to become passive investors. It is possible to recognize this early in life and change your life so you can be financially independent from a paycheck.

Paying for Expenses:

With your personal life, there are two kinds of expenses: fixed expenses and variable expenses. Fixed expenses are your rent, mortgage, car payment, utility bills; and the variables are food, clothing, transportation, and doctor visits. These expenses are based on need. You should have a budget for these expenses and pay out of your income on a regular and consistent basis. However, when you buy a TV, furniture, rugs, appliances, dishes, or go on a vacation, you pay for it out of your savings or from left over paycheck money after you have paid and planned for all your needed expenses. You need to understand the difference between the two because this is where most people make mistakes and get themselves into trouble.

Paying Taxes:

Paying taxes is a fact of life. Everyone has to pay a portion to their city, state, and the federal government. Taxes are calculated based on your income. The more income you have, the more taxes you pay. However, there are other ways to use more of your money for yourself through separate business entities and leave your money for yourself instead of giving it to the government. The government pays a lot of tax incentives and tax credits for those who risk their money and start their own businesses, hires employees, create jobs, and spend money on buildings, equipment, and technology. After all expenses and exemptions that a business can declare, there are not many taxes that the business entity pays. You can take advantage of the same opportunity if you form a business of your own.

7th – Treasure of Wealth – Work Sheet:

I will pay myself in these ways:

_____

_____

_____

I will add additional income in the following ways:

_____

_____

_____

I will pay off my debt in the following ways:

_____

_____

_____

I will read the following books on money management:

_____

_____

_____

I will invest for my retirement and emergencies in the
following ways:

_____

_____

_____

I will become obsessed with generating passive
income from these sources:

_____

_____

_____

These are my fixed expenses:

_____

_____

_____

These are my variable expenses:

_____

_____

_____

7th –Treasure of Wealth – 7 Daily Reminders:

1. Money is my friend and is there to serve me.

2. Think of creating passive income.

3. Spend less than your current income.

4. Pay with cash or debit card for your shopping.

5. Think of saving and protecting your assets.

6. Prevent late charges and extra hidden fees.

7. Shop for lower priced cable and telephone services.

In Conclusion

Thank you for taking the time to read this book. Your time is valuable and to spend it on anything that is not the best is not in your best interests. If you have learned one thing from this book and accepted it as a change in your lifestyle for the better, I accomplished my mission. I am humble and grateful that I was able to share this knowledge with you.

Please visit www.farimawassel.com and subscribe to get the latest and small tips and tricks that will make your life easier and happier. For questions and comments, please contact me at 7tPress@farimawassel.com or connect with me through:

Facebook.com/FarimaWassel

Twitter: @/FarimaWassel

YouTube.com/FarimaTV

Recommended Reading:

Frank Tibolt, "A Touch of Greatness"

Stephen R. Covey, "First Things First"

Stephen R. Covey, "The 7 Habits of Highly Effective People"

Robert G. Allen, "Creating Wealth"

Gerald G. Jampolsky, "Love is Letting Go of Fear"

David R. Hawkins, "Power vs. Force"

Andrew Weil, "Spontaneous Healing"

Phil Laut, "Money is My Friend"

Robert T. Kiyosaki, "Guide to Investing"

Michael E. Gerber, "The E Myth Revisited"

Timothy Ferriss, "The 4-Hour Workweek"

Bob Proctor, "The Secret"

Dr. Laura Schlessinger, "The Proper Care & Feeding of Husbands"